One Tree Hill
to Brockley Green

by
Anthony Watson

First edition March 2018
Second edition December 2018

With the exception of pages 3, 30, 33, 38, 67 and 84 all unattributed
images are from a collection belonging to the author.

First published in March 2018 by
Anthony Watson
E-mail: rosandtony@ntlworld.com

ISBN:
978-0-9956726-0-4

Text set in Times
© 2018 Text by Anthony Watson
Second edition by Ash Print Ltd, Sundridge, Kent TN14 6EE

To Rosamund

Preface

The author of this book grew up locally during the nineteen forties, fifties and sixties. Then there were many older citizens in their seventies and eighties, who had been born in Victorian times, and would recall the days of their youth. A Miss Hamilton who attended as a child, Queen Victoria's Diamond Jubilee and remembered the days before Stondon Park was built. Mrs. Merryfield, who recalled looking from her house across open land to Brockley footpath and memories of Noakes Farm. The milkman who recalled parts of the Croydon Canal and the gentleman who as a teenager took part in the One Tree Hill Riots in 1897. The lady who was a maid at Brockley Hall and whose husband went to school with the son of the gardener, also my old neighbour who had worked at the firework factory, and still made firework cases at home for Wells Fireworks. All of them unwittingly were sketching out an outline of history in my mind, eager to search out their life and times, having given me leads to pursue. I owe them much, and I am glad I listened to their old tales.

One Tree Hill

In centuries past the thickly forested woods to the southeast of London provided an ideal environment for recreation, and doubtless some very fine views were to be taken from its many hilly districts. King Henry V111 used to frequent the area of Shooters Hill, (known to this very day as Crown Woods). An interesting account is given in Hone's Day Book :

"Henry V111, when young, delighted in much pageantry, and the early part of his reign abounded with gaudy shows; most of them were of his own devising, and others contrived for his amusement. Among the latter we may reckon a May–Game at Shooters Hill, which was exhibited by the officers of his guard; they in a body, amounting to two hundred, all of them clothed in green, and headed by their captain, who personated Robin Hood, met the King one morning as he was riding to take the air, accompanied by the Queen and a large suite of the nobility of both sexes."

May Day for centuries, has been a time of great importance in the English calendar and even up until the beginning of this century, the festivities spilled over from country to town and the suburbs of London.

In Old and New London one reads, "In the neighbourhood of Peckham Rye, on the road to Forest Hill and Sydenham, is a hill with an oak upon its summit, called "Oak of Honour" at present shortened into "Honour Oak". It is said to be so called because Queen Elizabeth, in one of her excursions on horseback from Greenwich, dined beneath its shade. The original tree has long since perished, having been struck by lightning, but it has been replaced by a successor. Mr. James Thorne, in his "Environs" writes:- "In the chamberlains papers for 1602 is this entry 'On Mayday the Queen (Elizabeth) went a-maying to Sir Richard Buckley's, at Lewisham, some three or four miles off Greenwich.' Buckley's house was probably on the Sydenham side of Lewisham, where is Oak of Honour Hill, so named, according to local tradition, from Queen Elizabeth having sat beneath the oak on its summit when she went hither a-maying."

Councillor Nisbet described Oak of Honour Hill at the turn of the nineteenth century "Roque in his map of 1745 delineates the hill as rough and unprotected waste, with cultivated lands running up to the east, north and western base. Such was its appearance at the beginning of the last century, (1800) when the cornfields of Brockley Hall farm extended to the eastern, and Homestall farm to the northern slopes of the hill. The London to Croydon canal, which opened in 1805, ran past the southeastern foot of the hill, and a lock called top lock, existed near the point at which the Honor Oak Park railway station is now situated. Many persons still living remember the lock, over which was erected a foot bridge connecting a path running from Forest Hill Road over the crown of the hill and on to Brockley Road. This path was crossed by a stile at its commencement in Forest Hill Road, by another stile near to the canal, and by a third at its termination at Brockley Road. Another path ran from Peckham Rye, along the east side of Priory Farm, and adjoining with another coming from the direction of Nunhead went up the northern slope of the hill, at the top of which it formed a junction with the path from Brockley to Forest Hill Road, already mentioned. All these paths were crossed by stiles. The hill was at the commencement of the last century (1800) used as a semaphore station by the Honourable East India Company, to signal the appearance of their vessels in the channel. It was also put into requisition by the Admiralty at the time of Napoleon Bonaparte's threatened invasion of England."

For many years, the Oak of Honour had been a meeting place for beating the bounds of the Camberwell Vestry. On such an occasion it is recorded that on 11 May 1899, members of the Board of Overseers and local authorities, gathered by the Oak and sang together Psalm 100. Apart from a cottage built for the semaphore staff, the only other building near the summit of the hill was St. Augustine's Church, built in 1872/3 on a site given by Mr. Edwarde Clarke of Oaklands, Forest Hill Road. The clay hillsides were the source of hundreds of loads of clay taken by Mr. Marshall, for pottery and brickmaking in Forest Hill Road.

In 1896 much of the Hill was leased to a golf club, and a six-foot high fence was erected, enclosing the land. This caused outrage as many people regarded the land as an open space. A number of meetings protesting against the enclosure, were held in the spring and early summer of 1897, on Peckham Rye, and resulted in the formation of The Enclosure of Honor Hill Protest Committee.

Mr. S.E. Adams, proprietor of the Samuel Bowley Coffee Tavern, provided room for the first meeting of the protest group, which took place on 6 August 1897. The following officers were elected, Mr. J.C. Jones, Chairman; Mr. Goddard Clarke, J.P.and London County Councillor,Treasurer and Mr. J. Nisbet Honorary Secretary.

The committee of the twenty three members at the first meeting quickly grew to one hundred and fifty, many of them being members of the Camberwell and Lewisham local authorities. The Lewisham members formed a sub committee with a number of residents from Brockley and Forest Hill, with Mr. W.J. Gilham as the Honorary Secretary.

The campaign to secure freedom of the hill was supported by the Commons Preservation Society represented by Mr. L.W. Chubb, Secretary.

Much time was spent searching the archives of the Record Office, the Board of Agriculture, and the British Museum, as well as visits to the House of Lords, the offices of the Admiralty, the Customs House, the local authorities of Camberwell, Deptford, Lewisham and Woolwich and the County Offices at Maidstone and Kingston. Indeed anywhere that might provide supportive evidence of rights of way over the hill. When the evidence had been collected and collated, the Enclosure of Honour Hill Protest Committee approached the committees of Camberwell and Lewisham that had been formed to enquire into the protest, and a conference was called for 28 October 1897.

As no practical progress appeared to have been made towards the immediate removal of the fences, the general public grew more restive. Further, the Golf Club Authorities prosecuted two lads for breaking down of fences and trespassing on the hill on Monday 23 August 1897; they were later convicted and fined. This caused much indignation. The Brockley News reported:-

"On Saturday evening (2 October) the Protest Committee held an open air meeting at the corner of London Road near Forest Hill station. Mr. J. Wilde presided, and addresses dealing with the matter (Honor Oak Hill) were delivered by Messrs Glanville Morrison, (Bermondsey Vestry) J. Hamden Davis (Camberwell Vestry) Gregg (Lewisham) and others, and the following resolutions were adopted:-

'That this meeting of residents of the district regrets the loss by enclosure of one of the most healthy resorts in the neighbourhood, and hails with pleasure the action by the Protest Committee in the work they are doing to secure this interesting and beautiful spot once more for the people's use'.

'This meeting offers its sympathy to the parents of George Geffrey and Percy Armstrong, for all that the lads have undergone through defending what we consider to be a groundless charge of destroying some fencing said to be the property of a golf club on Honor Oak Hill, on Monday August 23, and we trust that their innocence may yet be proved to the satisfaction of the Home Secretary. Further, that copies of the resolution be sent to the Home Secretary and the Members of Parliament of Lewisham and Camberwell.' "

On Sunday 3 October, a meeting of the E.H.H.P.C. was held on Peckham Rye, and as a result of an amendment to a resolution of confidence, a motion was carried which authorised the removal of the fence (by force) the following Sunday. Events were moving too fast and in an unconstitutional way, and so the Protest Committee wrote to the press disassociating itself from the proposed assault.

Councillor Nisbet described the scene. "On Sunday 10 October there assembled at various points in the vicinity of the hill, in the afternoon, expectant crowds aggregating fifteen thousand persons, who, for some time, waited patiently for the appearance of the appointed demolisher. Some of the more adventurous losing patience, began attacking the fence on Honor Oak Park, pulled down a section, and entered upon the hill. This proved the signal for a general rush from this point, followed by another rush from Honor Oak Rise. The hill was covered with a disorderly multitude, and it was quickly

found necessary to reinforce the police who had been posted to keep order. An attack meanwhile, was made upon the cottage occupied by the ground keeper, whose wife at the time, was lying seriously ill in the house; considerable damage was done to the premises, and would have proved more serious, but for the timely arrival of a number of police who, with some difficulty, kept the crowd at bay."

Efforts were made by some of the more orderly to draw the

masses away, an impromptu meeting was called to this effect, and a member of the Vestry, Mr. J.E. Gregory, and others addressed the crowd and called for calm. The crowds resumed a less violent attitude, and joined in singing "Rule Britannia, Britannia Rule The Waves" and then dispersed quietly.

During the following week, the Golf Club issued a notice to the press through its solicitor Mr. Claude M. Treadwell, pointing out that the land owners from whom they had been given the lease, had a valid title to the area, and the Golf Club would not fear to face a judicial enquiry.

The following Saturday Messrs. Ben Ellis, Frederick Polkinghorn, Herbert Triggs, Charles F. Hawkin and Henry Martin went to One Tree Hill, and by prior arrangement in the presence of Major Gilbert of Scotland Yard, Superintendant Carr, other police officers, and officers of the Golf Club, pulled down a section of the fence wide enough to drive a cart through and proceeded on to the hill. Thereupon their names were recorded so that the Golf Club might make a prosecution if they should wish to do so. It was generally understood that the proceedings were undertaken in order to give grounds for a legal decision on the question of trespass. There was no ill feeling about the action, rather a friendly understanding about the matter. The events of the following day, however, were conducted in an entirely different humour, as the enclosure protest became increasingly bitter.

The Brockley News, 22 October 1897 :- " As expected by the police, there was serious trouble on Sunday. The police, however, had made preparations accordingly.

As early as nine o'clock in the morning police were drafted into the district. Some were lodged in the Golf Club pavilion, fifty were placed near St. Augustine's Church, fifty more in two empty houses near Honor Oak station. The police were drafted in small batches, so as not to attract particular notice, and they were practically in hiding. Sections continued to arrive up till two o'clock, and the total number was about two hundred foot police and twenty mounted men. They were skilfully posted by Major Gilbert and Superintendant Carr. The crowds began to gather at two o'clock. An hour afterwards there were at least five thousand persons on the Honor Oak Rise side. By half past three, the numbers were nearly as great on the St. Augustine's Church side.

Spectators were taking up special positions. Every window commanding a view of One Tree Hill was filled with onlookers, and at every street door, persons were gathered, eagerly discussing the prospect of a row.

It was nearly half- past three when the rioting began, by an onslaught at the entrance gate of the Golf Club, by a crowd of young roughs. Young men most of them, many of the loafer class, but there was a fair sprinkling of thoroughly respectable people drawn there out of curiosity. An organised rush was made at the gate at the top of Honor Oak Rise. The police were drawn up in lines, two deep, outside the gate. They stood the first rush, were then borne back, and it looked as if they could not withstand the onslaught. Then one man seized a portion of the fence to tear it down. Firmly, and without undue violence, Police-Inspector West forced him back. Almost immediately, the inspector received a terrible blow on the head. The man was arrested and forced towards the gate.

A cry of "rescue" was raised, and an attempt at rescue was made. Stones, large–sized flints were flung at the police. The mounted men came up, and their horses, like the men, were made the targets for the stones and sticks of their attackers. The attempt at rescue failed, ...two men arrested were taken within the enclosure, the mob meanwhile hooting, yelling, and hissing. The police simply pressed the mob back, forcing them down the Rise slowly but steadily. But the attacks on them continued, and a charge of the mounted men was needed. The police by four o'clock had carried out successfully their manoeuvre of clearing Honor Oak Rise, at the bottom of which they posted a strong line of patrols. Here thousands of people were kept constantly on the move by the mounted police.

On the other side of the hill, however, the fight raged stronger still. There was another swaying mob, howling and screaming. There were many police, foot and mounted men. Surrounded by the mob, they were often attacked singly and in couples, heavy sticks were frequently used to belabour them, stones and half bricks were thrown by the hundred, short sticks whirled through the air, and frequently found their mark. A police officer's face was cut with a stone, so was the face of a journalist, for the Press men there, all of whom had been admitted to the hill, aroused the resentment of the mob as much as did the police. Police Inspector Knighton got a very ugly cut, and further arrests followed. Between half-past three and half-past five ten arrests were made. These arrests, absolutely necessary as they were, infuriated the mob more and more, though it taught some of the crowd a lesson. At half-past five a great blaze was seen. The furze had been fired, and it was pretty evident that the fire had been deliberately lighted. The flames rose two yards high and burned fiercely and rapidly in the direction of St. Augustine's Church. There were in the crowd many who thought matters were getting too serious, and they helped to stamp out the fire. They had only succeeded in subduing it when a second fire was lighted, bigger than the other, and starting as the other had done with flame of a fierce nature, conveying the impression that oil must have been the substance used to create the conflagration, and supplying proof of organised incendiarism. This second great bonfire burned itself out partly, but had only just subsided when a third fire arose. The police at last decided there had been enough of it, and proceeded to clear the large field which rises from the Forest Hill Road to St. Augustine's Church. It took a lot of clearing, for the force was not large (enough) to deal with a crowd so great, so excited, and so vindictive. It took a full half-hour, from half-past five to six, to get the field cleared, but the task was at last effected and the troubles for the day were over. The public houses opened at six o'clock, the 'opening' helped the police amazingly."

At Greenwich police court the following day various persons were charged with offences arising out of the Sunday Riots, at least two were sent to prison, and others were fined. Writs were issued by the Forest Hill and Honor Oak Golf Club against Mr. Ben Ellis and his four companions who had pulled down a portion of the fence in Honor Oak Rise the previous Saturday.

The Times three days later reported the following threatening letter:-

"Mr. Claude M. Treadwell Hon. Solicitor to the golf club at One Tree Hill, has received a letter from " Brockley Rise" dated "14.10.97" informing that he "must look out; the

CLUB HOUSE, HONOR OAK AND FOREST HILL GOLF CLUB.

ground can go, but you will have to look after yourself at 'home'.

This is no joke; you brought it about with Mr. Neil, so you can blame yourselves. As for the Sunday's work, I was there, and the crowd behaved very well until the police interfered. The idea of locking up boys. They were afraid to take hold of the men whom (sic) were leading the boys. I may tell you there will be more than stones and sticks later on; perhaps a little bit of lead will fetch some of you to your senses and let the public have their rights, which they intend to have and will eventually. Believe me, you're not safe nor is the judge for his hard sentence." The letter is signed "One of the Public".

On the following Sunday 24 October, a crowd of over 10,000 gathered in the afternoon on the hilly ground by St. Augustine's Church. No attempts were made to break the fences around the hill, and the six hundred police who had been drafted in found little to do and the crowds dispersed as the evening drew on.

This was the last major public gathering, on the hill, and ended the short-lived policy of trying to reclaim the hill by force. On 10 October, some success had been gained in obtaining mass access to the grounds. On 17 October, despite much violence, no attempt succeeded in obtaining access, and many were doubtless shocked by the retribution of the courts. By 24 October, it appeared that all violent means of destroying the fences had been abandoned, though the size of the crowds showed there was still considerable interest in the affair. However it seemed all that human muscle could do to reclaim the prospect, for the general public, had failed. But that was not the end of the story.

The original Protest Committee, who had involved themselves purely with peaceful agitation, had been extended to include representatives from both Lewisham and Camberwell. Having considered the position after the recent rioting, they issued the following notice through the press and on posters and handbills:-

"The recent disturbances on One Tree Hill render it necessary for the committee to appeal to all thoughtful citizens, to support them in their endeavours to obtain the restitution of Public Rights by legal and constitutional means, and to abstain from forcible action, which may alienate public sympathy and jeopardise the issue. The policy of the Protest Committee, taken in conjunction with the public authorities, in obtaining the necessary evidence, is the surest method of securing One Tree Hill for the people.

In prosecuting the necessary enquiries, searches are being made in the Public Record and Government Offices, Museums, Libraries, etc., and a large mass of valuable information has been obtained from old residents. Any precipitate action is deprecated, and should be carefully avoided."

Winter passed, however, and summer came, another winter passed and summer came, winter passed and another summer came; committee meetings, further discussions, reports, joint committees, another winter, another summer, no right of way, no public access, no recreation, and just as surely, still no one would give up, or give in. There was a determination, that somehow, a way would be found for the subjects of the kingdom to sit at leisure, where Queen Bess had sat, so many years before.

Evidence of five Rights of Way and witness from eighty seven persons had been documented. Twenty of them were selected to appear before the joint sub-committees of Lewisham and Camberwell during the winter of 1897/8.

On 26 January 1899, the Honor Oak and Forest Hill Golf Club succeeded in prosecuting five men for trespass and damage. On 25 March 1899, the Joint Committees agreed to take legal action, the two authorities agreeing to pay fifteen guineas costs each for legal

St. Augustine's Church circa 1905

expenses. The counsel appointed by Lewisham and Camberwell authorities reported that it could only find substance in two Rights of Way: Brockley Road, crossing the old canal at a point where the Honor Oak Park railway station now stands, running up and over the hill to Forest Hill Road, and another path which started at Peckham Rye, and running along the east side of Priory Farm, to a point at which a railway arch is now situated, went to the top of the hill, where it joined the former path to Brockley.

The evidence for these two paths, however, was not considered strong enough for the legal experts to recommend action by the Joint Committee. The Commons Preservation Society, had reported the following:- "The preservation of Honor Oak Hill has occupied the attention of the Committee. The hill itself has become somewhat notorious owing to the rioting with which the assertion by the public of alleged Rights of Way running over the hill was accompanied. Injunctions were subsequently granted against the several defendants who asserted the rights of the public. As they possessed no funds, appeared in person, and made claims which it was palpable it would be impossible to substantiate, it cannot be said that the case for the public was placed before the courts in a favourable manner; a Joint Committee, consisting of representatives appointed by the Camberwell Vestry and Lewisham Board of Works, is therefore considering the matter. The Society has been able to assist the Joint Committee by advice, but whether the right of the public to use the paths can be substantiated or not, it is eminently desirable that the land should be preserved as an open space; it would seem to be preferable to acquire the whole of the hill than to fight an action the result of which would be doubtful.

The Hill has been under the observation of the Society for some years, as forming one of the most desirable open spaces in a portion of the Metropolis which is becoming rapidly built over, and it is hoped that the Local Authorities will see their way to initiate a scheme for the purchase of the land."

During the period since the One Tree Hill enclosure had begun, there had been a reorganisation of local government, and the subsequent change of borough boundaries brought the whole of One Tree Hill into Camberwell. Mr. Tagg, the Town Clerk of Camberwell, at the suggestion of Mr. Chubb, the Secretary of the Commons and Footpaths Preservation Society, approached through a third party, Mr. T.E. Ward the owner of the hill, with a view to purchasing it as an open space.

Mr. Ward agreed to sell at a price of not less than one thousand pounds an acre. However, this the authorities declined to pay. Furthermore at about this time they managed to acquire most of the land surrounding the hill, sixty acres, at five hundred and fifty pounds per acre, from the northern slopes to the Brockley footpath.

In 1902 a clause was inserted in the London County Council General Powers Bill for the compulsory acquisition of One Tree Hill, and passed the Parliamentary Committee on Bills on 24 February 1902. With the owner still unwilling to sell at a price agreeable to the council, the case was sent for arbitration. In December 1904 the counsel for Mr. Ward agreed to accept six thousand one hundred pounds from the Borough of Camberwell for the fourteen and a half acres of land.

Monday 7 August 1905, was a warm, bright, sunny day, with glorious blue skies.

A perfect day for a Bank Holiday. From the brow of One Tree Hill one could see right across London, and beyond the many London landmarks (St. Paul's Cathedral, Houses of Parliament, Tower Bridge) to Middlesex and Essex. In the other direction the Downs of Kent and Surrey were not beyond perception. It was a panorama that at last could be enjoyed by everyone, for this was the day that One Tree Hill was to be officially opened to the public.

Thousands of holiday makers climbed the slopes to see the opening ceremony. The presence of the Camboro' Band engendered a truly jovial spirit. From a platform bedecked with the choicest municipal bunting, in the company of at least thirty six Aldermen and Councillors, Mr. L.W. Chubb, Secretary of the Commons and Footpaths Preservation Committee, and surrounded by all those who had taken part in the long agitation for the public rights of way over the hill, the Chairman of the One Tree Hill Protest Committee, Henry Robert Taylor, L.C.C. (ex Mayor of Camberwell) declared the space open to the public.

Amid much cheering Mr. Chubb gave thanks to Miss Octavia Hill, who had donated one thousand pounds towards the cost of acquiring the land.

A beautiful address illuminated on vellum, ornamented with an oak tree and oak leaves was presented to Councillor John Nisbet, Honorary Secretary of the Protest Committee. The Chairman, Henry Robert Taylor, with the assistance of Mrs. Taylor and John Nisbet, planted a young oak tree near the spot where Good Queen Bess had sat so many years before.

A few feet away there remained a stump of a previous oak marking the spot. A circular seat was erected around this, and on the backrest a plaque with the inscription:

A circular seat with plaque around the old oak's stump and a new tree.

"This seat, placed upon the sight of the old Oak of Honour, was presented by Alderman J.G. and Mrs. Hichisson, of Wells Street, Camberwell and Belmont Park, Lee, to commemorate the restitution of this beautiful and historic resort, to the public use, for ever, on 7 August 1905."

ONE TREE HILL

Lets's twine a laurel wreath for those
To whom the debt is due,
And write each name on deathless scroll
In letters bold and true.
For ne'er did fight for land and right
The heart of London thrill
As did that grand, historic rush
That won us One Tree Hill.

They sowed a seed that Sabbath day
That's blossomed into life:
They smashed the planks of legal cranks
Of grabbing and of strife.
And while a tree or hill shall stand,
They'll, tell as years roll by,
The stirring tale of One Tree Hill
That looms o'er Peckham Rye.

M.A. O'C.
South London Press

Image courtesy of Southwark Local History Library and Archive

Open Day celebrations and Octavia Hill, the lady in a white blouse seated.

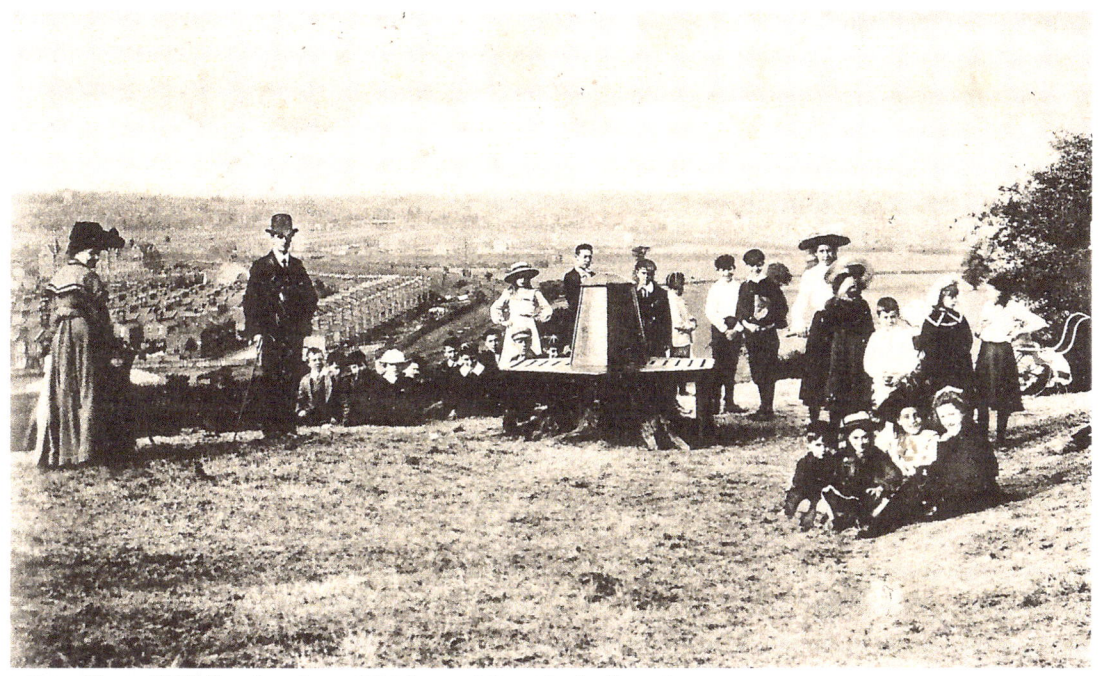

One Tree Hill Park, circa 1905, and Ivy Dale Road.

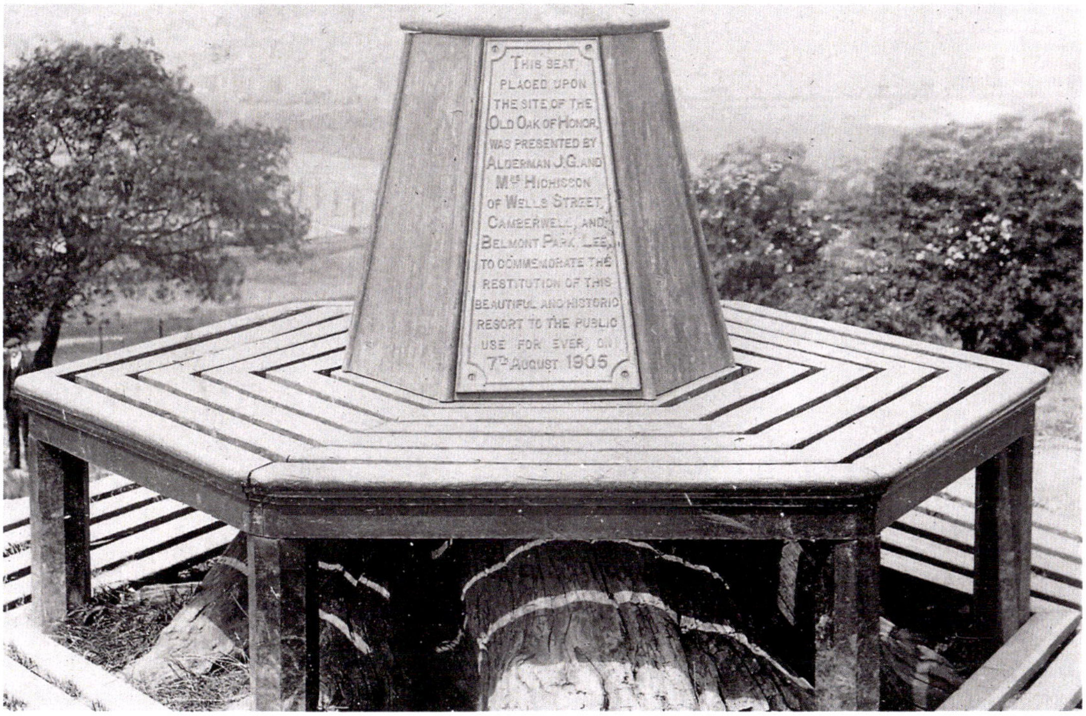

Image courtesy of Southwark Local History Library and Archives

A circular seat was erected around the stump of a previous oak - the fourth to mark the spot.

The golf club pavilion about 1904

The Putting Trophy for 1928

Golf Club Button

The Forest Hill and Honor Oak Golf Club continued until 1952, in later years as a nine hole course.

Wells of Honor Oak

In 1881 the London Brighton and South Coast Railway Company opened a new station at the foot of Oak of Honour Hill, from which the area now takes its name, Honor Oak Park.

Honor Oak Park was then sparsely populated, the only buildings being a few large Victorian residences claiming the magnificent views to be had along the side of One Tree Hill, (formerly St. Germains Road, after the Earl of St. Germains, the land owner of much of the area, later renamed Honor Oak Park) the well known church on the hill, St. Augustine's built in 1873 and a number of dwellings in Devonshire Road. The remains of the old Croydon Canal could still be seen at this time. The back gardens of the houses from number 95 Honor Oak Park onwards ran down to the canal, each having a footbridge at the bottom of the garden, over the water, to gain access to the tennis courts beyond. To this day the gardens of Boveney Road, which were built on the tennis courts, appear in two levels, the higher level being the earth filled canal bed, the course of which can still be seen. The whole of the area to the east of Honor Oak Park, between the station and St. Augustine's Church was farmland, dotted with ponds which were the remains of the canal. It was this piece of land that was to become the site of an old established family firm, whose products were utilized not only in the two great wars, but in countless open air festivities and celebrations, bringing colour, brilliant spectacle, and luminous displays to countless thousands, the like of which may never been seen again. It was here that Joseph Wells junior was to pass on through his son and grandson, the family business of Joseph Wells & Sons, Firework Manufacturer, Illuminator, Public Decorator and Limelight Contractor, at Honor Oak Park, for over half a century.

It was in the 1830's that the foundation of what was to become one of the premier firework companies, grew out of the business which Joseph Wells managed near Millwall on the Isle of Dogs. He was an explosives lighterman, having a fleet of barges transporting gunpowder and Chinese crackers. Gunpowder was greatly used not only by the Navy and the Army, but also for domestic purposes. Gunpowder could be purchased from ironmongers shops, and ignited in the coal fireplace, the vibration from the bang, being effective in displacing the soot from the chimneys, especially of copper clothes boilers, used in the kitchens of so many houses. The use of barges for bulk transport of explosives was appropriate as the railways had yet to design the special gunpowder wagons which were to be used in later years.

Joseph Wells interest in pyrotechnics, commenced with the manufacture of ships signal rockets, and red flares and blue lights, believed to have been used by ship's pilots. This proved to be such a success that he later opened a factory at Earlsfield, alongside the river Wandle. There, fireworks were made not only for Guy Fawkes night, but also designed for public displays, such as the International Exhibition in 1873 where Joseph Wells was awarded a Gold Medal for Superiority of Signal Rockets.

The business continued to diversify and Wells came to add the names of Illuminator, Public Decorator, and Limelight Contactor to that of Firework Manufacturer. He contracted to

TELEPHONE Nº 504 SYDENHAM.   TELEGRAPHIC CODE A B C 5ᵀᴴ EDITION.

Joseph Wells
AND SONS
CROWN BRAND

PYROTECHNISTS
25Y TO 12Y
EARL'S COURT
EXHIBITION,
EGYPTIAN
GOVERNMENT.
ALEXANDRA PALACE,
ROYAL
BOTANICAL GARDENS,
WINDSOR CASTLE,
&c &c

CORONATION
PRICE LIST
OF
UNSURPASSED
FIREWORKS.

CHIEF OFFICES
AND
FACTORY
HONOR OAK PARK, LONDON.

ESTABLISHED
1839.

Walter Mills

CABLES & TELEGRAMS WELLS, HONOR OAK PARK, LONDON.

Image courtesy of Lewisham Local History and Archives

provide limelight illuminations for many London theatres and provided lighting for Lord George Sanger's Circus where he first met and became a great friend of Blondin, the world famous tightrope walker.

Joseph Wells died in 1874, but the company continued to prosper under the direction of his son, also named Joseph, and in 1875 was awarded the first prize for the finest Roman Candle at the Grand International Firework Competition at Alexander Palace. In 1891 the company was credited with a Diploma at the Royal Naval Exhibition and it was about this time that it moved its premises to Honor Oak Park. Joseph Wells obtained the lease of a piece of land on the lower slopes of One Tree Hill, where they sited their factory on 18 acres of the ground. The factory site was bounded on one side by the Honor Oak and Forest Hill Golf Club and on the other side by the London Brighton and South Coast railway.

The layout of the factory had to be planned to the satisfaction of the Home Office under the Explosive Factory Act 1875. In the early days of firework manufacture, there were small firework businesses, lacking in modern fire precautions, some even carrying out production in their homes, resulting in many accidents. There were explosions such as that at Madame Cottons factory in Westminster Bridge Road, and D'Anots factory in Lambeth. As a safeguard, the Explosives Factory Act of 1875 was introduced and brought all explosives manufacturers under the jurisdiction of the Home Office, and required all companies to be licenced.

The entrance to Wells factory, opposite number 95 Honor Oak Park, was obtained through two high wooden gates, adjacent to one of the street gas lamp posts, which of an evening, conveniently highlighted the name of Joseph Wells & Sons, inscribed boldly across the six foot doors. Inside the gates, a roadway ran the full length of the site, past the office and the buildings for paper case making, the chemical and miscellaneous stores, then turning right by the carpenters and wood store, the canteen, oblutions and stables for the horses, then leading to the left to run northwards down the centre of the site. There were three rows of buildings on the left and a row on the right of the roadway, twenty in all, built at distances of 25 yards apart, where the mixing of gunpowder and the filling of explosives were carried out.

Safety precautions, in which Wells prided themselves, required that only one person was employed in each mixing shop, and only four persons in each filling shop. Each building was constructed with a door at each end, to enable a speedy exit, and half way between each building was a metal 'flash' screen, so that in the event of an explosion or fire, the flames could not spread from one building to another, thus enabling any fire to be controlled. Further on were the packaging and despatch departments, and beyond that seven larger buildings, storage magazines in which the daily production was stored, and a gunpowder magazine. All filling sheds were allowed only 25 lbs of powder and filled goods at any one time, and the finishing sheds were only allowed 50 lbs of fireworks. Whilst this meant constant servicing of the workshops, collecting finished articles for storage in the magazines, and replenishing supplies, it proved to be extremely safe. All test work and proof firing took place at the extreme north end of the factory, and rocket testing carried out in the early morning before the golf course was open, the rockets being pitched over in that direction where there were no buildings.

Wells firework factory at Honor Oak Park

On many splendid occasions, streets and public and private gardens were decorated with the use of flags, fairy lights, bunting and Chinese lanterns by Wells of Honor Oak, such as the military concerts at Kneller Hall where Wells employees would create all the sound effects of a battlefield as a backcloth to such pieces as "The Battle Of Waterloo" and the "1812 Overture", as described in the Daily Telegraph, September 1910 : "Few scenes can surpass the loveliness of the gardens of Kneller Hall illuminated for a summer night's fete, and when the music of the band of the Royal Military School of Music adds its enchantment to the sight, and crowds of people, punctuated here and there with a scarlet uniform, beneath long festoons of lanterns, it would be difficult to exaggerate the attraction of this open air picture. Memories of the Crimean War were made doubly tender at this concert in view of the recent death of Florence Nightingale. Of the performance it is enough to say that the programme included overtures and selections by Wagner, Rossini, Gounod, Bizet and other composers, and came to a close with Eckersberg's Grand Fantasia "The Battle Of Waterloo". Fortunately the evening although without starlight, was fine enough to attract a large number of visitors; the air was windless, allowing thousands of fairy lights to shine with unfaltering brilliance, and an occasional flash of summer lightning relieved the darkness which encircled the gardens. Within them ample light was diffused from the coloured lamps clustered like jewels round the tree trunks and from the festoons of Chinese lanterns marking the limits of the enclosure. Ruby, emerald and topaz coloured glass was liberally used with beautiful effect for the lower lights, and the whole scheme of illumination, whether in

Image courtesy of Lewisham Local History and Archives

Wells Decorations at Kneller Hall

the sylvan parts of the garden, or by the edge of the water, was carried out with a taste and liberality rarely exhibited and always welcome in English open air fetes."

Wells displays became world renowned. They exported fireworks to South Africa, West Africa, South America, Australia, New Zealand, Iceland, Portugal, Italy and India with great success. They provided firework displays for the Turkish Government, the Belgium Marine Administration, the Royal National Lifeboat Institution, the Royal Botanical Gardens, Regents Park and Windsor Castle Empire Day celebrations. They were pyrotechnicians to Alexander Palace and to the Earls Court Exhibitions who wrote the following letter:-

The London Exhibitions Ltd.,

Earls Court
London S.W.

August 10th. 1910

Dear Sirs,

I feel it is only due to you that I should inform you how pleased my company is with the Firework Displays you have made here during the season. Not only were your prices reasonable, but the fireworks were of excellent quality and design, and gave pleasure to many thousands.

I hope our business relations will be renewed for many seasons to come.

Yours faithfully

On behalf of the London Exhibitions Ltd., Hemon Hart, Joint Managing Director.

Joseph Wells had two sons in the business, Joseph Christopher and Albert Edward. Joseph Wells died in 1912 and the business was carried on by them. In 1914 all production went over to Army Navy and Royal Flying Corps supplies and another factory was opened at Colchester in 1915 to keep pace with demand. Albert Edward took control of this plant. Joseph Christopher had four sons, Joseph Raymond, Albert Victor, Bernard William and Wilfred Denver. Joseph Raymond started work in the office early in 1915. Albert Victor started work at Honor Oak Park in 1917 on production. During the war the factory produced war stores; signal cartridges, signal rockets with various coloured flares for distress and code signals, smoke float boxes used for screening shipping during enemy attacks and float flares of 10,000 candle power. During the night a shipping lane would be made using float flares laid all the way from England to France. This illuminated channel was then safe for shipping to take supplies, as any protrusion in the water, indicating a submarine, could easily be seen in the light of the flares, by the patrol boats.

Picture courtesy of Lewisham Local History and Archives

Rifle grenades were also manufactured. These were fitted to a copper rod, which could be inserted down a rifle barrel and when fired burst at quite a height, and discharge a parachute with three lights hanging from it. These were used for coding signals, different combinations of colours, relating to a code, which was often changed two or three times a day, so as to confuse the enemy, giving troops in the field commands e.g. advance, retreat etc.

Wing tip flares were manufactured for the Royal Flying Corps. In the days before planes were fitted with electric lighting, these wing tip flares were fitted to planes wings and when ignited by electric impulse, lit up the ground as they came in to land.

Wells also made hand flares of red, green and blue, for ships in distress and signalling. Signal packs were also made for individual soldiers. Made of paper cases containing coloured stars like roman candles, they were self igniting. The soldier would press the case on to the end of his bayonet on the rifle, tear the tapes attached to the top of the signal and away went the shell producing coloured stars, so that he was always in a position, if isolated, to signal for help.

When the end of the war came there were great celebrations and Wells were asked to supply as many rockets as possible for a great display in Hyde Park. All available rockets were supplied, along with roman candles that had been stored in magazines since the beginning of the war!

After the war Wells turned to peacetime manufacture. Limelights were a thing of the past, electric spot lights took their place. Demand for illuminations, flags and bunting fell off, so they discontinued that part of the business. They concentrated on making display fireworks and smaller fireworks for November fifth, though the demand for all fireworks remained very high for the first few years after the war, having great difficulty keeping up with supply owing to the Victory celebrations which kept going year after year.

Wells company staff, creators of colour, excitement, spectacle, pictured at Honor Oak Park

Towards the end of 1922, Joseph Christopher Wells died at the early age of forty nine and Albert Edward became chairman of the company, which weathered the worst years of the depression. Many grand displays of fireworks were carried out at the Henley Royal Regatta, White City, Luna Park, Hyde Park, Earls Court, Wembley Stadium, Eton College 4 June Celebrations, Raneleigh Club, Harrow School, Windsor Castle, Cowes Royal Regatta and the Jubilee Celebrations of 1935.

At the Spithead Review in 1935, the ships were lined up row upon row, each with 150 rockets connected to electronic fuses. Twenty five thousand rockets, detonated by radio, were fired simultaneously in one breathtaking salvo.

About this time more advancements were made in prototype war stores. They produced a line throwing rocket called Trueflight that had fins attached to the tail and directed the rocket on a straight course so that it could drag a line from ship to ship, or ship to shore, which could then be used to feed a hawser. For airmen who had baled out into the sea, they made five star signals to be used from rubber dinghies, and illuminating cartridges for lighting up targets.

In 1937 Wells were informed that the lease at Honor Oak Park would not be renewed by Camberwell Borough Council when it was due to expire in a few years, also the lease of the factory land at Colchester had expired so they decided to purchase a new site at Joyce Green, Dartford, to bring the two factories at Honor Oak Park and Colchester together. The Colchester plant was in the process of being moved when the war began, but building carried on and the transferred Colchester factory was ready to commence production at Joyce Green in 1941. At Honor Oak Park, production continued. The day war was declared in 1939 they were in a position to manufacture war stores full time, and changed from peacetime manufactures to war supplies in one night!

During the war Wells produced yellow smoke candles, and identification flares, magnesium signal rockets, red and blue hand flares, and smoke floats. The smoke floats were made of balsa wood, and fired from a gun, created a smoke screen. They were used successfully in the North Africa landings. They made simulated gun flashes. Believed to have been used at El Alamein, the gun flashes were used during the night so as to deceive the enemy as to the whereabouts of the allies positions, thus enabling them to move position under cover of darkness.

Wells Fireworks also won a contract to manufacture a new invention, the photographic bomb. Albert Victor Wells recalls, "Doctor Coxen of Woolwich Arsenal had designed the photographic bomb, however Woolwich Arsenal required six months to manufacture them, so he came and put the proposition of manufacture to us. We promised them within a month. When the first six were complete I drove with them to Liverpool Street Station and put them on the train for RAF Mildenhall and two nights later they were dropped over Berlin. The pictures taken using the photographic bombs as illumination were perfect."

During the war Joseph Raymond Wells raised big companies of the Royal West Kent Home Guard and for this and other services received the M.B.E.

Honor Oak Park site had many hits by incendiary bombs, but the fires were kept under control and little damage was incurred.

In 1945 there was a run down in war stores production. They began to strip the buildings at Honor Oak Park in 1946, in preparation for transfer to Dartford, but firework manufacture continued for another year, the factory diminished in size, until one day in 1947, the doors to Wells of Honor Oak Park were closed for the last time.

Many of their employees moved with them, the last to retire in 1975. Albert Victor Wells retired in 1970, but continued to take a deep interest in all aspects of pyrotechnics, and to whom I am grateful for so much information, died in 1985. Bernard William Wells who began work at Honor Oak Park went to California in 1951 trading in fireworks in conjunction with the Atlas Firework Company. Joseph Wells' son Alan Wells, continued in the business for many years and has contributed invaluable material.

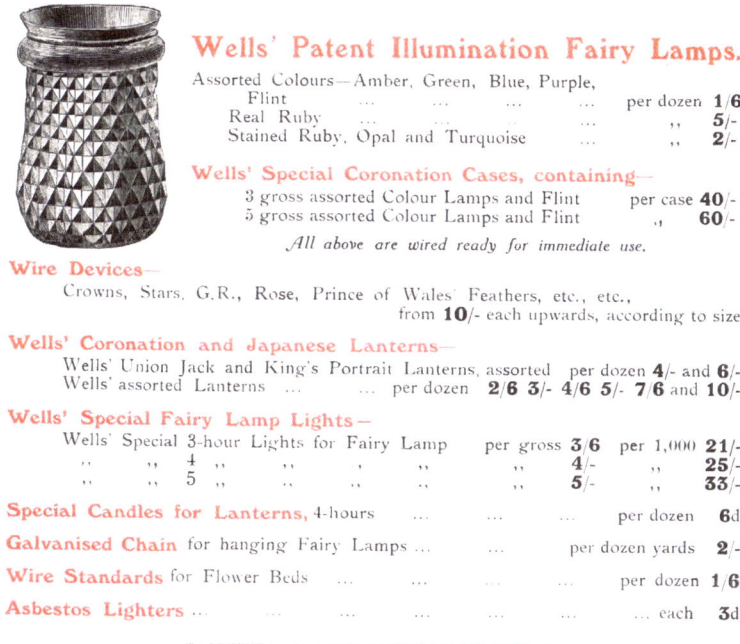

Wells' Patent Illumination Fairy Lamps.

Assorted Colours—Amber, Green, Blue, Purple,

Flint	per dozen	**1/6**
Real Ruby	,,	**5/-**
Stained Ruby, Opal and Turquoise ...	,,	**2/-**

Wells' Special Coronation Cases, containing—

3 gross assorted Colour Lamps and Flint	per case	**40/-**
5 gross assorted Colour Lamps and Flint	,,	**60/-**

All above are wired ready for immediate use.

Wire Devices—
Crowns, Stars, G.R., Rose, Prince of Wales' Feathers, etc., etc.,
from **10/-** each upwards, according to size

Wells' Coronation and Japanese Lanterns—
Wells' Union Jack and King's Portrait Lanterns, assorted per dozen **4/-** and **6/-**
Wells' assorted Lanterns ... ... per dozen **2/6 3/- 4/6 5/- 7/6** and **10/-**

Wells' Special Fairy Lamp Lights—
Wells' Special 3-hour Lights for Fairy Lamp	per gross **3/6**	per 1,000	**21/-**
,, ,, 4 ,, ,, , ,,	,, **4/-**	,,	**25/-**
,, ,, 5 ,, ,, , ,,	,, **5/-**	,,	**33/-**

Special Candles for Lanterns, 4-hours ... ... per dozen **6d**

Galvanised Chain for hanging Fairy Lamps ... ... per dozen yards **2/-**

Wire Standards for Flower Beds ... ... per dozen **1/6**

Asbestos Lighters ... ... each **3d**

Wells' Torches and Handlights for Processions, etc.

Prismatic Coloured Handlights, changing colour three times—
No. 1—½-lb. bore, 6in. long	per doz.	**4/-**
2—¾-lb. bore, 12in. long	,,	**8/-**
3—1-lb. bore, 12in. long	,,	**16/-**

Wax Torches, quite Clean and almost Smokeless. Specially recommended—
No. 1—Burning ¾ to 1 hour	per doz.	**4/6**
2—Burning 1¼ to 1½ hours	,,	**6/-**
3—Burning 1½ to 2 hours	,,	**9/-**
4—Burning 2½ to 3 hours	,,	**12/-**

These Torches are fitted with Wooden Handles complete.

Roman Flambeaux (Tin Torches)—
With Wick and Handle complete, as used in Tattoos and Processions.
On Hire ... ... **8d** each | On Sale ... ...**1/3** each

Balloons with Coloured Light attached, Red or Blue—
12ft. and Light ... ... **2/6** each | 20ft. and Light ... ... **5/-** each

The pictures on the following pages show the Croydon Canal in 1805 and a similar view in 1898 taken from One Tree Hill.

The bridge over the lock in the right of the colour picture was situated not far from what is now 95 Honor Oak Park, closing the top lock of the staircase of locks that enabled the canal to extend up the hill from New Cross. In the middle of the picture, in the distance, can be observed St.Mary's Church, Lewisham.

The sepia photograph circa 1898 shows bottom right the Forest Hill and Honor Oak Golf Club pavilion. The wooden huts beyond belonged to the Wells Fireworks Factory, and the gully in front of the site fence is the remains of the Croydon Canal. To the extreme left of the picture can be seen the back of the Brockley Jack and to its right St.Hilda's Church Hall. The houses under construction are in Stondon Park, and the fields beyond are part of the grounds farmed at Brockley Hall. One can see a few houses built in Holmsley Road, but Grierson Road and the turnings off and St.Hilda's Church were not built until some years later.

The dark line through the centre of the picture marks the hedged boundary of the railway cutting, and the bridge over it in the left of the picture (later taken down) known as Dead Bridge marks the top of what later became Courtrai Road, marked by an avenue of trees. Beyond in the distance can be seen St.Mary's Church.

CROYDON CANAL.
Depsford from the Lock keepers house.

View towards

H.Browne

A view of The Coydon Canal in 1805 probably painted from a point not far from what is now 113 Honor Oak Park. Copy of an image at the Museum of Croydon

View from One Tree Hill 1898

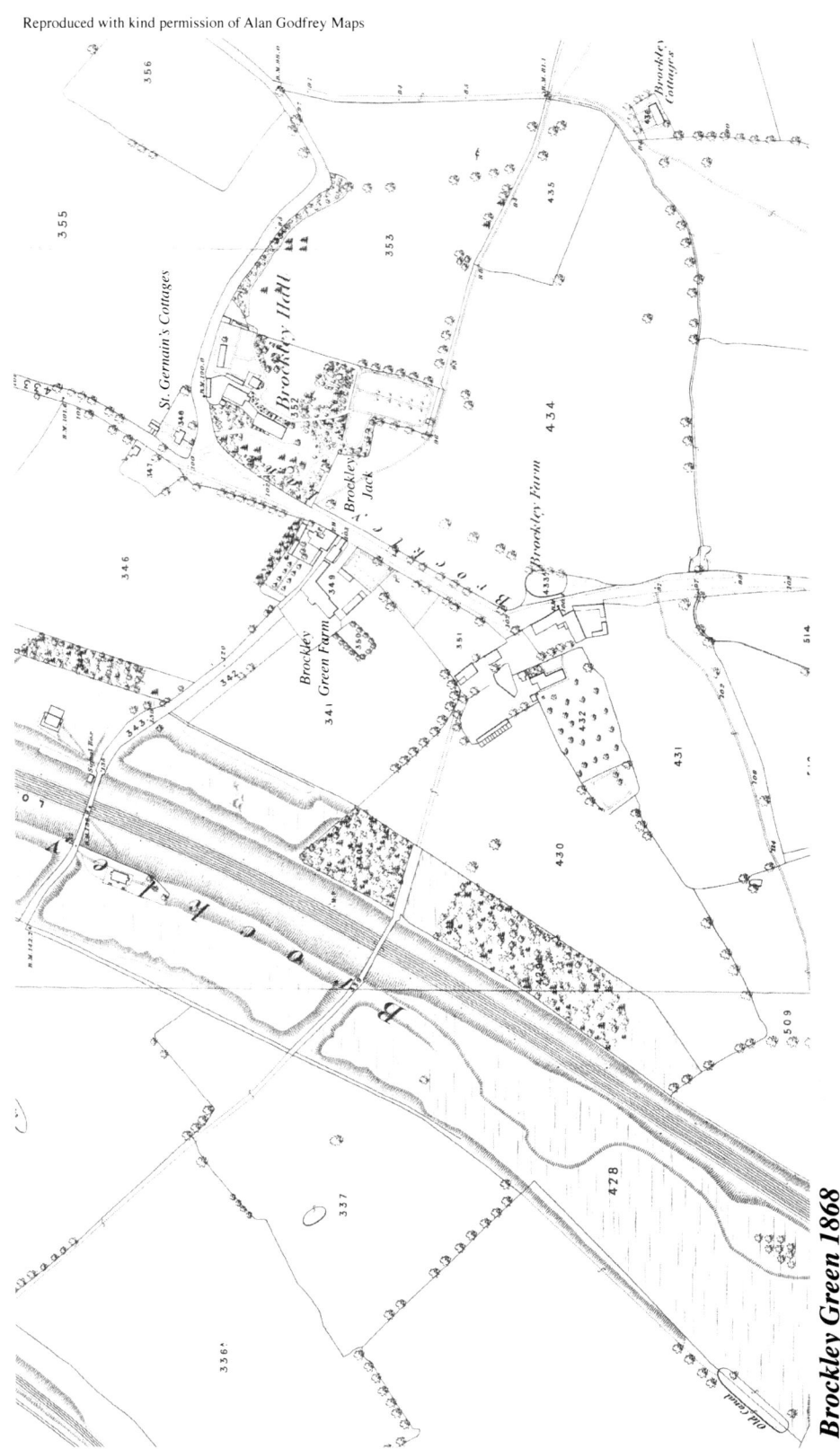

Brockley Green 1868

Honor Oak & Forest Hill
Golf Course

Wells Fireworks
Factory

Honor Oak Park
Station

Brockley Green 1914

Brockley Green Farm

The hamlet of Brockley Green consisted of Brockley Farm, Brockley Green Farm, The Castle Inn, Brockley Cottages, Brockley Hall and its staff cottages.

Brockley Green Farm, opposite Brockley Hall and adjacent to the The Castle Inn (later named The Brockley Jack) was occupied by George Colgate and his wife Jane. The 1841 census also shows his son, George, and daughters Ellen, Jane and Elizabeth and was also known as Colgate Farm.

George Colgate interested himself in public affairs, for many years, Liberal, with staunch 'Anti-State' principles.

On 26 September 1832 he chaired a meeting at the Rose and Crown public house Bromley, attended by interested parties who wished to see the abolition of Tithes. A resolution was passed promoting the establishment of an organisation to further that aim. The following January this resolution was adopted and a Bromley society for procuring the extinction of Tithes was formed. He edited a pamphlet "Tithe or no Tithes, that is the Question" a point upon which there had been much agitation in Kent, culminating in the 'Commutation of Tithes' Bill, being passed. During the campaign he wrote 9 April 1834, "I have this day had the satisfaction of having a fat lamb taken away for Tithe, having ten ready for the butcher".

George Colgate also held the title of Surveyor of Roads for the Parish of Lewisham for seventeen years, the first six gratuitously.

Picture courtesy of Lewisham Local History and Archives

Brockley Green Farm... "this quiet country place"

William Colgate

Image courtesy of Bessels Green Unitarian Church

George Colgate died at the age of 53 on 24 September 1847, and was buried at Bessels Green Baptist Chapel.

George Colgate was described as "a man of the very highest principle ….and of a remarkably serene temperament". Mrs. Elizabeth Love, of Filstone, Shorham, Kent knew him as being "Clear headed, upright, conscientious, eminently truthful and warm hearted, one who fulfilled every duty incumbent upon him; the love of the humorous was also a marked feature of his character. To know such a man was to respect and esteem him".

He was remembered by the poor he had cared for, a Mrs. Loft recalled "He was such a thoroughly kind hearted gentleman", William Morris remembered him, "He was a gentleman always, and so kind, I am sure he will go to heaven".

George Colgate had a cousin William, who at the age of ten, fled with his father and mother to America, as his father was to be summarily dealt with, owing to his sympathies with the right of labour and conscience, and becoming known as a "Tribune of the People" he earned the approbation of the government of the day.

In America, William took up employment in a New York soap, candle and starch company, and having learned the business, he branched out on his own account, founding what was to become the multi million pound business now famous for Colgate Toothpaste!

After the death of George Colgate, Brockley Green Farm was run by his wife Jane.

The 1851 census shows the farm as being of 95 acres and employing 5 labourers.

In residence were her son George 26 years old and four daughters Ellen 24, Jane 21, Elizabeth 16 and Julia 8. Also staying there as a guest of the Colgates was Elihu Burritt.

Born in New Britain, Connecticut on 8 December 1810, but owing to the sickness and death of his father when he was fifteen, Elihu Burritt had little formal education in his youth. He obtained work as an apprenticed blacksmith, and when funds and time permitted, he educated himself by borrowing books from his local library, which he studied at every spare moment. He mastered Latin,

ELIHU BURRITT

Greek, French, German, Spanish, Italian, Chaldia and Syriac and by the time he was thirty he could read over fifty languages.

This extraordinary talent made him famous. He found an outlet in giving lectures, especially on his pet subject, the brotherhood of man.

Having seen the Oregon crisis between the claims of England and the United States for land in Columbia, resolved peacefully, he was encouraged to exchange views with English pacifists. He visited England in 1847 and organised the League of Universal Brotherhood.

He published not only pamphlets and books on the theme of brotherhood, but also his journeys through England "A Walk From London To John O Groats", and "A Walk From London To Land's End And Back". He wrote 37 books including, "Sparks From The Anvil", and "A Walk In The Black Country".

He campaigned for the extension of the Penny Post to include overseas post, to encourage the interaction of different peoples. Eventually, Abraham Lincoln recognised his zeal for international relations, and made him United States Consular at Birmingham.

While he was visiting England in 1851 he befriended Ellen, Jane and Elizabeth Colgate who enthusiastically embraced his ideas through one of his Olive Leaf meetings. In his journals he refers to his visits to Brockley Green Farm, where he received hospitality and accommodation, and was appreciative of the Colgate's friendship. He kept a daily journal, in which he wrote the following :

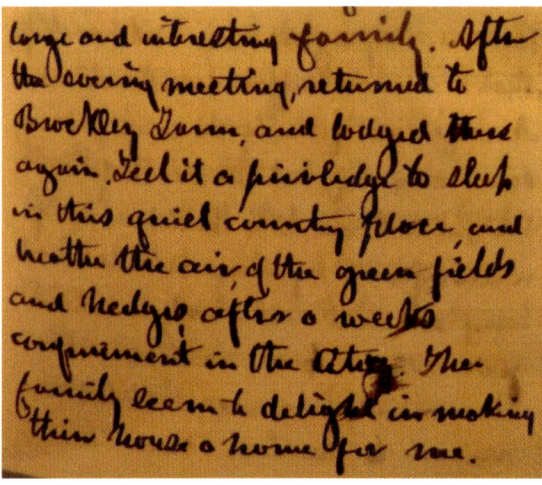

May 3 1850 "At 7 went out to Brockley Farm, and spent the night. Ellen and Jane (Colgate) are full of interest in the cause. It seems to be their life."

The next day: "......returned to Brockley Farm, and lodged there again. Feel it a privilege to sleep in this quiet country place, and breathe the air of the green fields and hedges, after a weeks confinement in the city. The family seem delighted in making their house a home for me."

In 1854 the niece of Elihu Burritt travelled with him to England where she spent most of her time in central London and she kept a daily journal.

Her name was Anna C. Strickland, and she describes her visits to the Colgates at Brockley Green Farm.

Of Sunday 29 October 1854 she wrote "Uncle (Elihu Burritt) and I went to Lewisham to Church (St. Mary's) where we met Miss Elizabeth and little Julia Colgate. They accompanied us to their home in Brockly *sic* a mile from Lewisham. It is a very interesting family, there being four daughters. Ellen the eldest reminds me much of my cousin Anna, Jane the next is full of animation and spirit which beams forth from her bright sparkling eyes. Elizabeth is as pleasant as the others, highly cultivated but perhaps not quite so lively. Julia the youngest is quite forward for her age, and plays on the piano admirably."

Monday 30 October 1854 "A most lovely day. Took a stroll over the field and hills with Elizabeth and Julia. When we returned they showed me their paintings and drawings which were most beautiful especially the fruit which looked so natural that they would most deceive anyone. The time seemed to pass away very fast and after bidding Ellen and Mrs. Colgate farewell, I walked to the station accompanied by Jane, Elizabeth and Julia."

At that time the nearest station to Brockley Green was Forest Hill. On Saturday 16 December 1854 she wrote "…..I took a train (from London Bridge) for Forest Hill where I arrived in about half an hour. Found dear Ellen (Colgate) waiting for me. After a long walk through a great deal of mud (it having rained the night before), we reached Brockley Farm".

Sunday 17 December 1854 "Went with dear Jane Colgate to the Lewisham Church and heard a sermon from the clergyman, Mr. Legg who I thought needed energy and more originality of thought."

Tuesday 19 December 1854 "A nice cold frosty morning, very much like our American weather. Although so very cold, yet we thought we ought not to neglect taking the fresh air. So after warming our cloaks, shawls and many other articles of clothing, dear Ellen, Julia and myself sallied forth and actually walked nearly three miles without stopping to rest. But this was not necessary as the cold bracing air gave us fresh energy and vigour. During our walk we took an imaginary sail up or down the canal. It would be difficult to tell which. This was accomplished by standing on a bridge which was over the canal and the singular appearance of the bridge & water by looking at the edge of them both makes it seem as if you were sailing."

Wednesday 20 December 1854 "Looking at the beautiful and accurate drawings and paintings which the Colgates do so nicely, has given me a taste for doing the same."

It is interesting to note from the 1861 census that Elizabeth and Julia Colgate were listed as 'Artist and Photographic Colourist.'

Tuesday 16 January 1855 "Uncle received a very sad letter from the Colgates, stating that they feared they should lose their brother, (George) who it was thought could not live throughout the day. He had always been an invalid and account when their affections had been entwined in the closer attachment. He was the only son of his mother and she an invalid."

Early on in her journals, Anna Strickland describes staying with the Robinson family and Mary Robinson at the Manor House, Crawley. The following journal entries show her renewing the acquaintance: Friday 1 March 1855 "In the morning Mary Robinson came.

It really does us good to see her again. We have not seen her since we left Manor House."

Monday 4 March 1855 "At 6 o'clock went with dear Mary Robinson to Lewisham where I expect to remain at her brother's for several days. As I have remained in London most of the winter, I thought that a change would do me good and could here see some of the sights around Lewisham. "

Tuesday 5 March 1855 "After breakfast, we visited Mr. Robinsons mill."

Mary Robinson was the sister of Joseph and Henry Robinson. Her brothers owned the business of J and H Robinson Flour Mill in Deptford. In 1866 Jane Colgate of Brockley Green Farm married Henry Robinson, and they lived at Cayuga House, Elliot Park, Blackheath.

Reproduced by permission of Historic England

The Mill owned by Joseph and Henry Robinson, the view from Deptford Creek 1883

Brockley Cemetery

Gravestone at The Unitarian Church, Bessels Green

Commemoration at The Unitarian Church, Bessels Green

Brockley Farm

Brockley Green circa 1845

The largest farm of Brockley Green was Brockley Farm, previously called Forest Place, or also referred to as Manor Farm. The 1851 census describes it as having 226 acres and the farmer as being Henry Owen employing nine labourers in addition to his own family. Living there at this time were Henry aged 39, his son Edward aged 13 and his daughter Emma and the sister of Henry Owen, Jane aged 40. Henry Owen's farm was also the postal address of his father's business, Owen and Sons, auctioneers, and later Henry Owen himself, auctioneer, whose advertisements of auctions appeared frequently in the press. However, it was an occurrence at Brockley Farm, a century before, whilst a Mr. Savage was farmer there, that the farmer was the victim of a gang of highwaymen, may have spawned the legend of the highwayman 'Brockley Jack' after whom the famous pub was named. In legend Brockley Jack was a highwayman who lived at the pub and went about his criminal activites, having placed an effigy of himself at a window, as an alibi. The London Evening Post dated 18 February 1735 carried the following report:-
"On Friday night last (7 February) five men masked came to the house of farmer Savage of Brockley in Kent, entered the same, and rifled the house of all the money and plate, and took each of them a shirt, which they said they were in great want of, they staid, *sic*, some time in the house, eating and drinking, and then went off with as much unconcern

as common visitors." In 1735, the renowned highwayman Dick Turpin, was engaged with others committing crimes in the vicinity of south London. In Captain Charles Johnson's 'Lives and Exploits of English Highwaymen' he describes how "Turpin with five others, in January, 1735 came to the house of Mr. Saunders, a wealthy farmer, at Charlton in Kent". They enquired if he was in, and as soon as he acknowledged their enquiry, they rushed in and tied him up, and his wife and some guests there. Turpin and his gang took a silver snuff box, upwards of a hundred pounds and other property including all the plate in the house. They fed their captives with wine and brandy and mince pies which they had found, and not withstanding the cries of a maid from an upstairs window, whom they suppressed, made off after two hours, into the night. Turpin's associates are listed as Fielder, Rose, Walker and one other making five.

It is next related how they raided a house in Croydon, belonging to a Mr. Sheldon. They found the coachman dressing his horses, bound him and then seized the master, and after treating him and his household the same way, they stole eleven guineas, and several pieces of plate, jewels and other valuable items. Before they left they returned two guineas and thanked Mr. Sheldon for his courteous manner! Charles Johnson goes on to describe how another highwayman, Henry Simms, known as 'Gentleman Harry' robbed a lady on Blackheath in her coach. About this time the 'hue and cry' was on for two groups of five highwaymen and the following reports appeared.

The London Evening Post February 15, 1735:-
"Yesterday (February 14) Sir Richard Brocas committed to Newgate four housebreakers, viz. William Williams, Richard Guilford, William Isaacson, and Robert Jacks, on the information of Joseph Cole, for being concerned with him in several felonies, robberies, and burglaries, in London and Middlesex; in particular, for breaking open a Silver Smiths shop in St. John's Street, and stealing fifty pounds worth of silver goods."

The Weekly Miscellany, February 22, 1735 :-
"The following is a description of some of the persons, not yet taken, who are charged by information upon oath, of committing several robberies and burglaries in the neighbouring counties, for apprehending of whom a reward of 50 *pounds* each is advertised in the Gazette.

Samuel Gregory, about 23 years of age, 5 feet 7 inches high, a long cut on his cheek, by trade a Blacksmith. He ravished the maid of Joseph Lawrence the farmer near Edgware.

Herbert Hains, a very pale man, about 25 years of age, wears a brown wig, about 5 feet 7 inches high, by trade a baker. Richard Turpin, very much marked with the small pox, about 5 feet 9 inches high, about 26 years of age, by trade a butcher. Thomas Roden, a little thin man, about 31 years of age, wears a light natural wig, by trade a pewterer." Whether any of these men were the ones who rifled the Brockley Farmhouse of Mr.Savage on 7 February 1735 has not been recorded.

"THE BROCKLEY JACK"
A BIT OF OLD LONDON.
The Oldest Wayside Inn. Near London.
Built Feb. 1398 • Demolished Feb. 1898.

In 1901 the firm of G. Weller & Co. of Greenwich, saddlers, issued a promotional calendar with the picture shown here, with the inscription 'The Brockley Jack Inn the Oldest Wayside Inn near London built Feb. 1398 demolished Feb. 1898.' It was indeed a structure of some antiquity, though it had not always been known as the Brockley Jack. The census of 1841 shows it as being called The Castle, and the landlord John Baker was still in charge of The Castle twenty years later when the census for 1861 was taken, and was still known by that name in 1871.

The Brockley Jack in the 1880's – still the leafy countryside.

By 1878 however, the name had changed to The Brockley Jack, as described in Butts Histrorical Guide to Lewisham:-'... "The Brockley Jack," a noted old hostelry, connected with Dick Turpin and fashionable dissipation of a bygone age. It is an old way-side inn, with outside a circular seat round an ancient elm tree, its upper branches being held together by an iron chain. The hostel has an outside bar, where the traveller can drink his measure of ale in the open air, or should he prefer it, mount the open staircase, and seating himself in the light gallery, observe at his ease, the carters refreshing themselves on the road. The more ancient part of this inn, which bore Dick Turpin's autograph, carved in the old woodwork, has been pulled down two years since, but even as it stands the hostel is a rare picture of roadside simplicity, and one of the very few remnants of past English life and manners.'

Like any old structure, doubtless its walls, if able to speak, would have many a tale to tell, and on more than one occasion was the nucleus of much villainy.

The Brockley Jack was also in the news on Friday 10 July 1885, the police discovered what they took to be a prize fight, behind the Brockley Jack. They found about 250 men had formed a ring and the pugilists were in the centre stripped to the waist. One of the contestants, John Parker, a known fighter, was later caught and committed to the Old Baily. The following summer, John Smith, better known as the prize fighter "The Greenwich Bruiser" was attacked at the Brockley Jack by several men, and again in Greenwich, and subsequently died of his wounds.

In 1893 the Police News for Saturday 25 March gave lurid accounts of the 'Brockley Outrage!' concerning little 10 year old Nellie Price who had been waylaid on her way to get some whiskey for her mother.

The Brockley Jack was also in the news on Friday 26 January 1877, when there was a notice of pigeon shooting to take place the following Sunday.

Under its new title of The Brockley Jack, the old inn became a place of recreation to the people of the expanding metropolis. Indeed by the 1890's when pristine new housing began to encroach on the green fields of the neighbourhood, it must have seemed at odds with its new surroundings. So many people made it their destination of inquisitiveness, that it must have been one of the most photographed of public houses. It was also the distant limit of the running circle of the Surrey Beagles. Their President was the Member of Parliament for Peckham, Mr. F.G. Banbury. The Illustrated and Sporting and Dramatic News for 1893 reported "The headquarters and starting point for ordinary runs is the Tyrrell Arms, Peckham Rye, thence the course is across the Rye past the Herne Tavern, along the Forest Hill Road, leaving Honor Oak Station, London Chatham and Dover Railway on the right, up the hill and over the steep rise called One Tree Hill, to Honor Oak Park, across heavy plough to the main road as far as the ancient and well known Brockley Jack, which marks the distant limit of the run, then into Mud Lane, and over more plough to Homestall Road, finishing on the east side of Peckham Rye."

At this time The Brockley Jack consisted of a small group of buildings. Looking at it from the front it was bounded on the left by the Brockley footpath which separated it from its neighbour where the Colgates used to live. Adjacent were the remains of a barn beneath which was a covered seat. The low building next to that housed a bar which

The Surrey Beagles and F.G.Banbury M.P. President

served beer from pumps beneath a window, through which ales were served. The trees in front had seats erected around them. An old tree had a dove house on a platform in the upper branches, lower down hung a whale bone with the words, 'The Brockley Jack', and a board showing the price of refreshments including luncheons. A sign on posts declared 'Billiards Best Public Table In Kent'. Finger pointers informed patrons that the billiards room was on the ground floor of the adjacent building, and that access to the gardens was under the covered stairway, which led to the upstairs refreshment room. The sign of The Brockley Jack, hanging from the tree was a whalebone and had originally been dug up in 1839 when digging the railway cutting, not far from what is now Honor Oak Park station. A painting of a lady in crinoline dress had been painted on it at some time, but later this was painted over and it was made into the inn sign.

To cope with the increased custom from London's ever expanding population, the Brockley Jack was pulled down to make way for a larger house of typical style. Many lamented the passing of this, the oldest wayside inn near London, where patrons could sample Noakes sparkling ales, reclining beneath the trees, enjoying the tranquil scene across the fields opposite.

The Brockley News of Friday 1 October 1897 printed the following lament by one, J. Lacy:-

'The Doom Of The Brockley Jack'

Four hundred years or more have passed,
And much I grieve to tell,
That thou, old friend, art doomed at last,
To take a last farewell;
But what of that, in love for thee,
I'm sure there'll be no lack,
But all will grieve to think we've lost
Our dear old Brockley Jack.

As years rolled on and love for thee
Stronger and stronger grew,
Till people flocked from far and near,
Their dear old house to view;
And still we grieve in heart and soul
And fain would see thee back,
But all in vain since none can save,
Our dear old Brockley Jack.

The history of thee, old house,
Has told a sadden'd tale,
How highwaymen and arrant rogues
Themselves did oft regale
Beneath thy roof and lay their plans
How they might rob and hack
Their victims as they ventured near,
Their dear old Brockley Jack.

But times have chang'd and neighbours meet
To tell their pleasing tales,
And oft in joyous song rejoice
O'er Noakes's splendid ales,
And never will our love for thee,
Old friend, one moment lack,
But all will grieve that we have lost
Our dear old Brockley Jack.

In late Edwardian times one of the out buildings at the back of the public house was the motor works of Earnest O. De Val. Earnest took an interest in the race to conquer the air. Whilst the Wright brothers had achieved flight in 1903, five years later, still no one had made a successful aeroplane here in England. Together with a gentleman named Mitchell and a Mr. Norrie, De Val constructed a monoplane in his works at the back of the Brockley Jack. The plane De Val and his associates constructed was of bamboo and canvas with steel strips to hold the bamboo together. The undercarriage comprised bicycle wheels with lengthened hubs mounted on a tubular frame. The aeroplane was powered by a 16 horse power racing engine. The wings were supported by wire bracing, and the rudder was pedal operated. The propeller was made of mahogany.

Image courtesy of British Museum Library

The Brockley Monoplane
Earnest O. De Val is seen here 5th from left, Mitchell 4th from left and Norrie in the pilot seat

In 1908 they took the plane to Abbey Wood, where other would-be aviators had attempted to become airbourne. At Abbey Wood they were hampered by rough ground, broken propellers and a weak undercarriage. The plane never did become airborne. Earnest O. De Val died in 1914, at the age of 44, his dreams of aviation unfulfilled.

Copy of a picture held at the Mary Evans Picture Library

Members of the Peckham Harriers running club in Mud Lane (between Brockley Green Farm and The Brockley Jack) 1891. Inset a club meeting.

The Brockley Jack circa 1897. I am grateful to David Hopkins for this picture which he resuscitated from an old glass negative.

Brockley Jack Inn 1897 by Philip Norman (copyright Museum of London)

Image courtesy of Ewbank Auctioneers, Surrey

This picture was painted in 1897 by Arthur Harding Norwood, who lived over the hill from the Brockley Jack, in Wood Vale, at the time of its demise. He had a passionate love for Kent and its countryside, which found expression in his paintings. His pictures came to adorn houses not only in Kent, but throughout the country, and reproductions of his paintings of places such as Knole Park and Penshurst on postcards, sold in their thousands. He seems to have been particularly interested in the picturesque Brockley Jack, for during its final days he photographed it on 27 September 1897 and again on 25 October and again on 16 November. These pictures can be seen on the following pages, along with his hand written comments.

45

The old "Brockley Jack" with its sign.   Arthur H Norwood.

From 27th Sep 1897. Powell & son, licensing holder.

14 Aug.   The sign on the old tree on the hill. "Brockley Jack" can be all out.

The old "Brockley Jack" from over the stile in the Lane

The ugly Lamp-post is not an improvement.

Andrew H Norwood.

Mon 25th Oct 1897. J.C.Q.

Brockley Hall

During the nineteen-eighties and nineties my wife and I used to spend many sunny summer days at the Post House at Stone in Oxney on the Romney Marshes in the hospitality of Mrs Margaret O'Connnor who had retired from being a postmistress, to providing bed and breakfast in the sixteenth century former post office building. It was probably at the time one of the quietest spots in Kent, and on a fine day, after breakfast in the garden, overlooking the meadows of sheep,we would take the footpath across the cornfield opposite and then across the next field, and through the wild flowered woods. Near the end of the woods could be seen Luckhurst Farm, a fine house and three or four dilapidated buildings, all of some antiquity. It is here that Humphrey Wickham (1777 to 1858) lived. In 1805 he married Mary Manwaring, and they had two daughters, Ann in 1807 and Elizabeth in 1810. Elizabeth married the son of William Noakes, called John Tompsett.

William Noakes who was born in 1784, lived for a time at The Colonels, Ticehurst. He married three times, Sarah Sawyer 1808, Ann Edwards Tompsett 1810, Mary Collins 1815. He had four sons, William born 1812, John Tompsett born 1813, Charles born 1819 and Benjamin Tompsett born 1828, and five daughters Sarah born 1808, Ann born 1811, Charlotte born 1819, Frances born 1823 and Emily born 1825.

John Tompsett Noakes, married Humphrey Wickham's daughter Elizabeth at the parish church of Stone in Oxney on 29 November 1836, and moved to 5 Claremont Place, Brixton, where they had their first daughter Pauline in 1837. John Tompsett Noakes is recorded as being a Hop Factor. They later moved to Harleyford Place, Kennington, where their second daughter Elizabeth was born in 1839, son Wickham 1841 then daughter Kate 1843 and John Tompsett junior 1844.

Luckhurst Farm, Humphrey Wickham lived here.

Image courtesy of Julian Noakes

W. & A. H. FRY, PHOTOS.   BRIGHTON

Elizaberth Wickham, wife of John Tompsett Noakes Snr of Brockley Hall

NIL DESPERANDUM

The Coat of Arms awarded to John Tompsett Noakes Senior of Brockley Hall in 1890 - Member of the Guild of Girdlers, Freeman of the City of London and member of the Merchant Taylors Company. The Coat of Arms carries the motto 'Never Despair'.

Brockley Hall in the 1860's

It was not long after this that the family moved to Brockley Hall, Brockley Green, where Ada Louisa was born 1847, Maud 1849 and the youngest son, Bertram in 1851. Members of the Noakes family resided at Brockley Hall for the next 85 years.

John Tompsett Noakes senior shared his time between that of business man, and gentleman farmer at Brockley Hall. He took a pride not only in the cattle he bred, which he exhibited at agricultural shows but also his gardeners were proud to exhibit at horticultural shows. John Tompsett's name appeared from time to time as the recipient for many awards for livestock.

Kent Cattle, Poultry & Implement Show 1859 - 'Pigs Best boar, T.J. Noakes, Brockley Hall, Lewisham.'At the same show "the bull of Mr. J.T. Noakes, Lewisham, was deservedly placed first. This fine animal, bred by the Prince Consort, was commended at Warwick this year, and has gained prizes at Dartford when 2 years 8 months old, and at Croydon when 3 years 2 months. He is a bull of great size and substance, extremely level, and girths 8 foot 2 inches."

The following year 1860 it won Special Prize, for Bull of any age, of a pure breed, open to all England.

In July the same year an award under Class 2 Boars of a Small White Breed "John Tompsett Noakes of Brockley House, Lewisham, Kent, 10 months 3 weeks, 4 days, bred by exhibitor."

In the Kent County Agricultural Show of 1861 award for "Best Cow in Calf to Mr. J.T. Noakes Brockley Hall, Lewisham." and "Best Cow or Heifer under three years old, - 2nd to Mr. J.T. Noakes of Brockley Hall." "Best Yearling Bull to Mr. J.T. Noakes, Brockley Hall."

At the Lewes Fat Stock Show 1864 "To the owner of the best open Heifer, bred anywhere, Mr. R. Sharpe, East Grinstead, bred by Mr. Noakes, Lewisham."

In 1865 the cattle plague spread throughout the country. The Rinderpest as it was known, accounted for at least quarter of a million deaths in cattle. Once infected a herdsman could expect to lose up to 95% of stock. Naturally farmers were eager to find an antidote. When the herd of shorthorns owned by John Tompsett Noakes became infected at Brockley Hall, the action he took to combat the disease seemed to be so effective that he wrote to the Times newspaper, and other newspapers and periodicals reported it.

He worked on the assumption that the infliction caused fermentation of the blood, and after treating some of the herd on this assumption, the cattle that he had instructed to be given a solution of hyposulphate, survived.

His experience was recorded by many journalists, but there appears to be no scientific records of the results of the treatment. To what extent the cattle at Brockley Hall were eventually affected is not known, but there are few reports of his well known shorthorns appearing at cattle shows thereafter. Certainly, he had plenty to occupy him with his brewing business interests.

A Preventive Treatment of the Cattle Plague.

[FROM *Bell's Weekly Messenger* OF JAN. 15.]

MR. J. T. NOAKES, of Brockley, Lewisham, Kent, who is well known to most of our readers as a breeder of shorthorns, has communicated to us the particulars of a system of preventive treatment which in his own herd, and in the herds of a few neighbours to whom he mentioned the system, has proved eminently efficacious. The mode of treatment is founded on the assumed fact that fermentation of the blood is essentially the nature of the disease. The antidote is hyposulphite of soda. The herd at Brockley, before the introduction of the plague, consisted of valuable high-bred shorthorns and ordinary farm stock. The disease first manifested itself in one of the latter, having been conveyed, it is supposed, on the clothes of a man who had been in contact with infected stock on another farm, where several cows had died. The herdsman then had the directions for treatment furnished to him, but he treated only the pedigree cattle. These, although no provision for isolation was attempted, all escaped contagion, while every one of the ordinary stock, which had not been subjected to the treatment, died, The alleged specific is simply hyposulphite of soda, 5 lb. dissolved in 100 gallons of cold water, which thus impregnated should be the ordinary drink of the cattle so long as danger of infection remains. In order to test in the severest possible way the efficacy of this mode of treatment, a cow which had been subjected to it was placed among a number of infected animals, without receiving the slightest harm, and is now in perfect health. There is no risk of injury, Mr. Noakes states, attending the use of hyposulphite of soda according to this prescription, and the preventive may with safety be administered even to young calves in their milk. The ordinary price of hyposulphite of soda is about 6d. per lb. ; but wholesale it will not cost more than 20s. or 22s. per cwt. The manner of application, too, has the merit of simplicity, and the preparation involves but little trouble. Attempts to *cure* may do harm, by conducing to the spread of infection ; endeavours to *prevent* disease are not open to this objection. We earnestly recommend a full and fair trial of the treatment, and hope that any of our readers who may adopt it will not withold from us the results for publication.

In Victorian times the hamlet of Brockley was in an area designated as West Kent, which sported one of the oldest cricket teams, dating back to 1711. On 18 July 1868, West Kent cricket club played Beckenham winning by 79 runs on the first innings. The scoreboard looked like this:-

WEST KENT

F.N. Steatfield, c Day, b Chalmers ....10 runs

J.B. Martin, b Day 0

E. Norman, b Day 5

E. Lubbock, b Chalmers..6

P. Thresher, c Day b Chalmers 4

A. Lubbock, not out 69

H.W. Richardson, st A.C.Wathen, b W.H. Wathen......................29

P. Norman, c A.C.Wathen, b Day 13

H. Gosling, c and b Day 1

B. White, b Day 7

F.J. Edlemann, b W.H. Wathen..0

W.E. Denny, b Day...2

Of the eleven wickets, Frank Day took no less than seven! He was described as "a rather good fast bowler, and a kind unassuming man, who also played for the Crystal Palace Club, and was a partner in the firm of Day, Noakes & Sons, brewers, Bermondsey.

Frank Day's father Robert Day had been in business as a maltster in Westerham, Kent, and acquired with Charles Payne and Henry Spike, interests in the Black Eagle Brewery, Whites Grounds, Bermondsey in 1848, including buildings and plant, horses and two houses and tenements.

Charles Payne died four years later, and not long after, John Tompsett Noakes became a partner. The acquisition of White's Grounds brewery meant that Day could brew both types of beer, using the hard London water to brew Porter, and the soft Westerham water to brew Pale Ale. Noakes being a Hop Factor made the partnership in the brewery a natural progression. Robert Day, retired in 1860, his son Frank taking his place. In 1864 the partnership with Henry Spike was dissolved and the company became known as Day, Noakes & Sons.

In 1848 the brewery had a chain of 23 public houses, spread over a wide area, including some that were to become notable, such as The Red Lion, Grange Yard, Bermondsey; The Crown and Anchor, Old Kent Road; The Dartmouth Arms, Forest Hill; The Three Tuns, Beckenham; The Crown, Sundridge Park; The Porcupine, Mottingham; The Red Lion, Plumstead; The George, Beckenham.

Picture courtesy of Bromley Local Studies and Archives

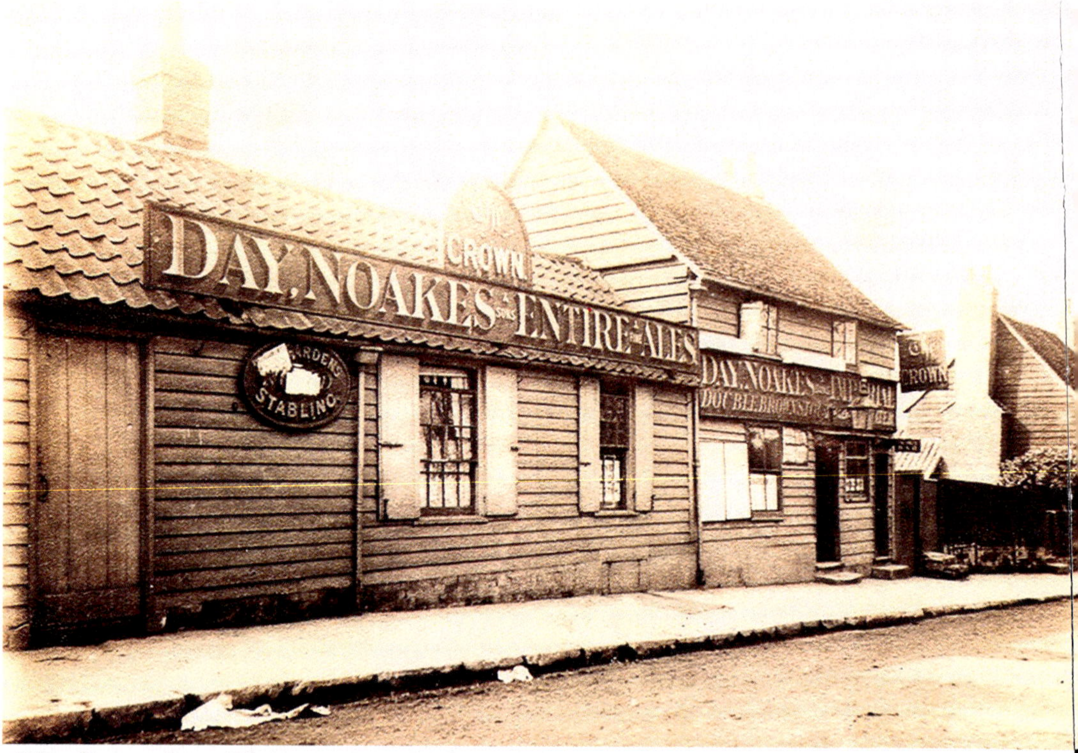

The Crown Inn, Plaistow, Sundridge Park

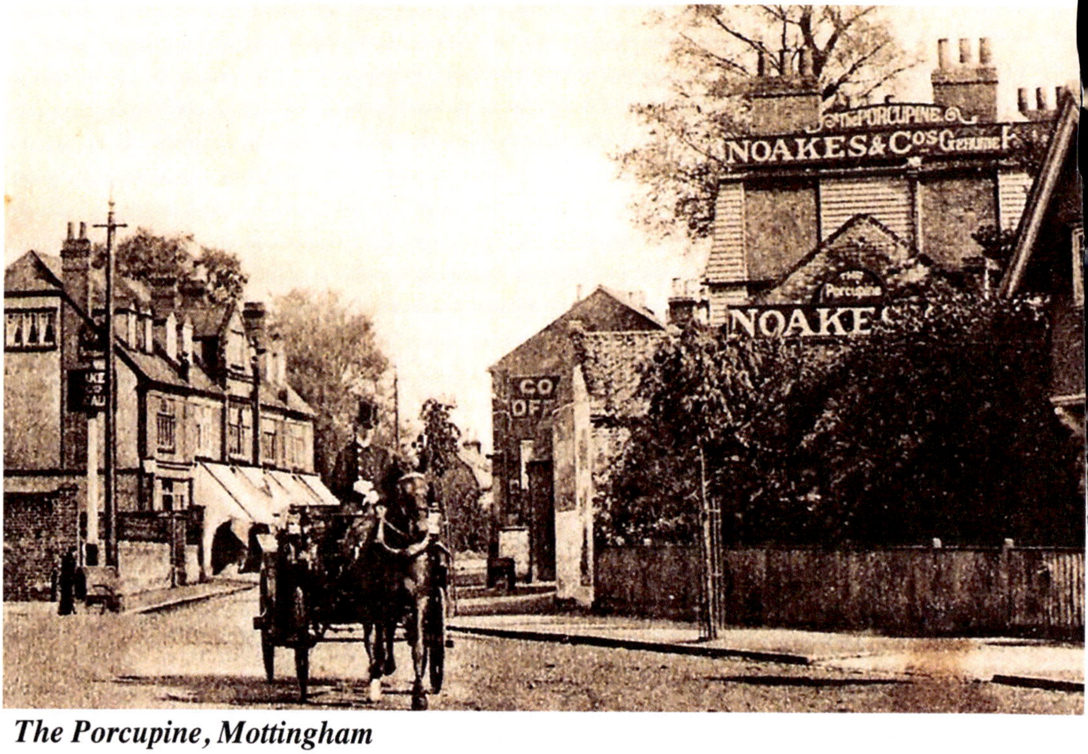

The Porcupine, Mottingham

Wickham Noakes in about 1863

In 1857 John Tompsett Noakes arranged for his eldest son Wickham to begin a seven year apprenticeship with William Robinson White, Merchant Taylor and Hop Factor and later Wickham joined his father in the brewing business. The partnership John Tompsett had with his brother William as Hop Factor was dissolved and John Tompsett shared the business of Hop Factors with his youngest son Bertram. In 1865 Wickham married Kate Francis Shorter of Oakfield, Honor Oak Road, at St.Mary's Church, Lewisham. They crossed the threshold of their new house Fairfield, The Avenue Beckenham, newlyweds. At their residence at Beckenham, Wickham and Kate Francis had eight children. Wickham

Fairfield, 11 The Avenue, Beckenham, in 2011

Francis in 1866, John Norman 1867, Mabel Kate 1869, Evelyn Beatrice 1870, Sydney Neville 1873, Millicent 1874, Stuart Bertram 1875 and Marie Lilian 1878.

As London expanded the company grew, and more and more pubs were added to the portfolio. Over the next thirty years the chain of premises expanded to over 100 outlets, and Noakes became a household name on the high street. In 1896 John Tompsett Noakes died leaving his interest in the Whites Grounds brewery and the pubs to his son Wickham and his interests in the Hop Factors, by then in Southwark Street to his youngest son Bertram, and his property at Brockley Hall to his five daughters and Bertram.

The brewing empire continued to expand under the direction of Wickham Noakes. Wickham Noakes launched Noakes and Company Limited on the stock exchange in 1897, buying out the ownership of Day, and brought three of his sons, John Norman,Wickham Francis and Sydney Neville into the company as directors. Many of the public houses were rebuilt and expanded, the brewery of Neville Reid, Thames Street, Windsor was purchased in 1918 and Cannings brewery, Peascod Street, Windsor, which held a Royal Warrant, in 1920. These takeovers extended Noakes business in the expanding suburbs west of London, beer being provided from the Thames Street Brewery. The Noakes empire eventually expanded to 280 public houses.

Oakfield, Honor Oak Road, Kate Francis Shorter, the daughter of John Shorter lived here. She married Wickham Noakes in 1865

Copy of an image held at the Museum of Croydon

Buoyed by the new business prosperity, Wickham Noakes purchased Selsdon Park House, near Sanderstead at the turn of the century, where he enjoyed the life of the country gentleman. In 1903 The Sketch publication devoted its cameo 'Beautiful Homes And Their Owners' to Wickham Noakes of Selsdon Park, where he employed a butler, two footmen, two ladies maids, a cook, three housemaids, three kitchen maids, and a hall boy to cater for the needs of his family. His son in law Charles Cooper Austen became estate manager with a separate staff to manage the estate which covered 679 acres.

The views from the house which faced towards the Surrey Downs, were magnificent. An old elm planted by Queen Elizabeth I many years before, and the various coloured flower beds, sloping terraces, and copper beeches, graced by winding shady walks, added elegance to the grounds. A cricket ground supplied much recreation and near a picturesque old water tower, stood an archway which once formed part of the thirteenth century Blackfriars Monastery .

A gamekeeper was employed to oversee the woods and manage the pheasantry, all well stocked with game, for a grand shoot to celebrate his birthday each year in November. There was a billiard room, with a high Tudor ceiling, once a chapel, from which could be seen through large glass doors, the Winter Garden, with its foliage and palms. The Lounge Hall held many ancient weapons, helmets, armour, stags heads and other hunting trophies. Over the panelled oak staircase, and in the light from a huge stained glass window, hung pendants emblazoned with his Coat of Arms.

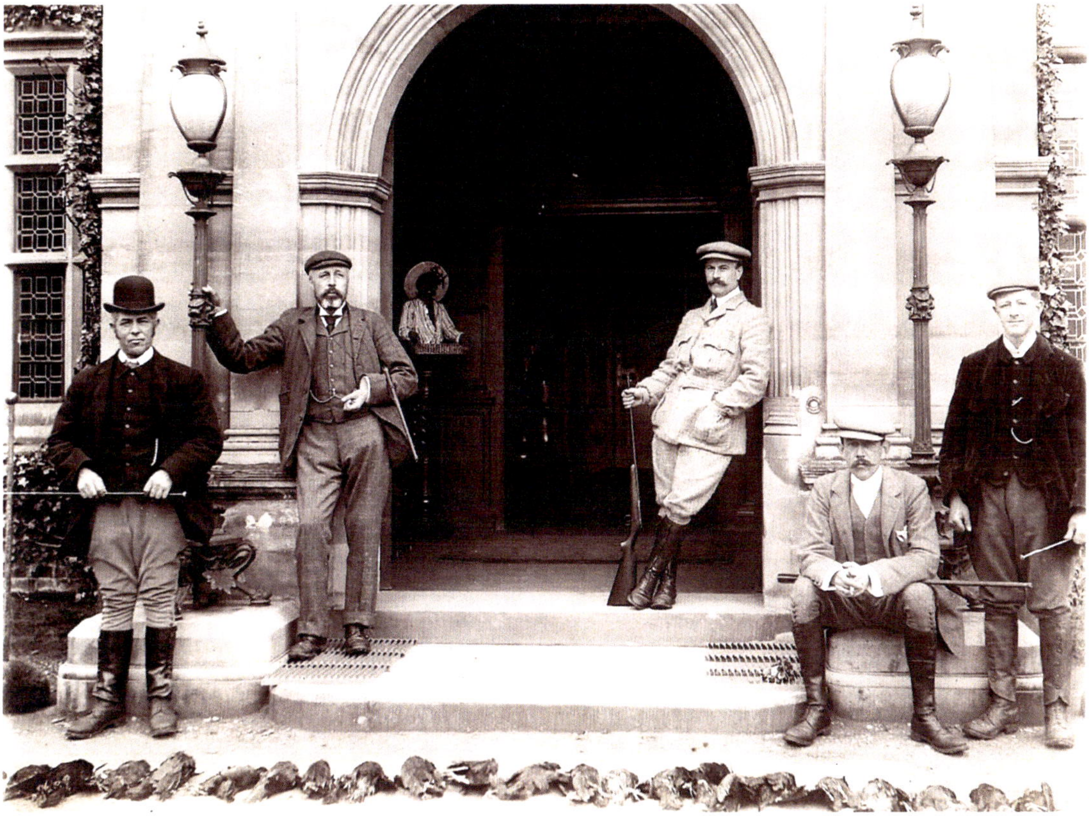

Image courtesy of Marigold de Jongh and Lesley Yeo

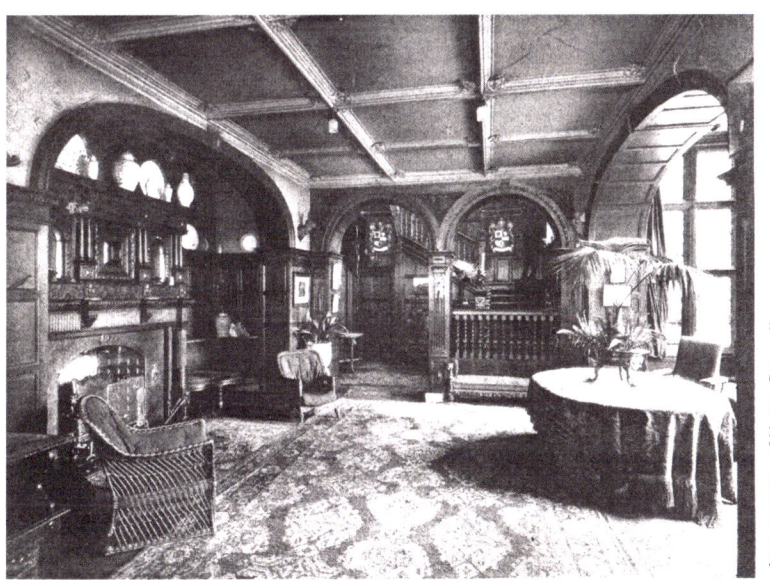

Pictured in the Sketch 1903 'Beautiful Homes And Their Owners' Wickham second from left. His Coat of Arms was also embossed in the brass fire surround of the Lounge Hall below. Second from right Wickham Francis Noakes.

Image courtesy of Norma Cornwell

Image courtesy of Norma Cornwell

Wickham's Coach, horses, trumpeted heralds, coats of arms, uniformed footmen, heraldic leopards

Image courtesy of Nobby Seymour

Wickham Noakes was made High Sheriff of Surrey in 1907, and sported the Coat of Arms he had inherited from his father, not only on banners in the house, but on the family china, and his carriages and attendants. Here he enjoyed the fruits of his business success, and all seemed set for a blissful residence.

Wickham (centre) wearing his uniform as the High Sherrif of Surrey 1907

Advertisement c.1904

In 1909 however his wife died and was buried in the nearby churchyard at All Saints Sanderstead, but Wickham continued to live at Selsdon with his son Sydney Neville and his daughter Maria Lilian. Three of his sons continued to prosper as directors of Noakes & Co. but the fourth and youngest, Stuart Noakes, educated at Rugby, became a Member of the London Stock Exchange in 1899.

The following is an extract from The Stock Exchange Memorial Book:-

Image from Stock Exchange Memorial Book

CAPTAIN STUART BERTRAM NOAKES, Royal Army Service Corps, was the youngest son of Wickham Noakes of Selsdon Park, near Croydon.

Born in 1876, he was educated in Rugby, and on leaving went on the Stock Exchange, where he become a Member in 1899.

When taking a detachment out to Egypt on the R.M.S Aragon, he was drowned, the ship torpedoed off Alexandria on 31 December 1917.

Image courtesy Marigold de Jongh and Lesley Yeo

Sidney Neville Noakes 1872-1921

He is also remembered on the War Memorial at Alexandria, the War Memorial at All Saints Churchyard, Sanderstead and on a plaque in the church.

Image courtesy of Nobby Seymour

John Norman Noakes in 1905

Just five weeks later, Wickham's second son John Norman, also a great sportsman who suffered from epilepsy, died suddenly at Selsdon Park on 4 February 1918. He was just 51 years of age.

The eldest son, Wickham Francis, married Edith Constancia Stephens, at St. Peter's Church Brockley, in 1893. He succumbed to tuberculosis, and died at his residence Pencroft, Redhill, on Christmas Day 1918, the third son to die in twelve months.

Wickham Noakes in 1918

There remained only one son to succeed his father, and to share his grief. Sydney Neville Noakes was born in 1872. He shared the love of hunting, shooting and fishing of the rest of the family, and contributed to the number of inanimate birds, animals and fish that adorned the house, the ample grounds of Selsdon being a playground for such a sport. Whilst out hunting at Selsdon in the summer of 1921, the gun he was carrying, discharged accidentally when he was crossing a stile, delivering a fatal shot. That final fatality, on 1 August 1921, left Wickham Noakes with no sons to succeed to the estate. He died two years later on 6 September 1923, his final years being sad and melancholy. He was the eldest and most successful son of John Tompsett senior.

Image courtesy of Julian Noakes

Tompsett's second son, born 1844, was named after him, John Tompsett Noakes junior. JTN junior was only 18 years old when he left the family home at Brockley Hall. He married Barbara Ann Hunt at St. Saviours Church, Southwark. The following year she bore him a child which sadly died. JTN junior then left England, alone, never to return. He went to live in Onehunga, New Zealand, where his aunt Ann Eliza and uncle Dr. Walter Harsant lived. Three years later he married Susan de Berri and brought up a family of six, Bertram de Berri, John Francis, Hugh Lionel, Esther Maude Olive, Louis Norman Guy and Edith Ivy at Inkerman Street, Onehunga, Aukland.

John Tompsett Noakes Junior

John Tompsett Junior's residence, Inkerman Street, Onehunga, Aukland, New Zealand.

The youngest son of John Tompsett Noakes senior, Bertram, was born at Brockley Hall in 1851, and lived most of his life there. He was indentured to his eldest brother Wickham, who was ten years his senior, in 1866. He served the standard apprenticeship of seven years and like his father and brother became a member of the Merchant Taylors Company, having his freedom bestowed in 1873 and livery in 1876. He was a partner in the family firm of J.T. Noakes, Hop Factors at 8 Southwark Street.

Having spent most of his life as a bachelor at Brockley Hall, he married Florence Ann Hayward in the summer of 1910 and made a home with her at Tierney Road, Streatham. They lived there until her death in November 1919, thereafter he lived at Brockley Hall until he died in the summer of 1922.

A Business Card

Croquet at Brockley Hall, circa 1865.

A Noakes family photograph. The lady at the back left is unknown. The others from the left are Ada Louisa, Pauline, Maud, Elizabeth their mother, Bessie (Elizabeth) Kate and Bertram

The pictures of the ladies of Brockley Hall on the previous pages were probably taken in the 1860's. Here can be seen the mother, Elizabeth Noakes and her five daughters, the eldest Pauline, Elizabeth, Kate, Ada Louisa and Maud. During the 1850's they were educated at home by their resident governess Louisa Belgrave, a member of the Belgrave family who had left England to settle in Barbados. In 1861 the older sisters along with their brother John Tompsett Noakes, enjoyed the whole summer on the Isle of Wight, staying at The Royal Pier Hotel, Ryde, in early June and then The Bonchurch Hotel, for the rest of the summer. The Misses Noakes as the five sisters were referred to, had the benefit of the sea air in October 1865, staying at 11 Grand Parade, Eastbourne, with their parents, John and Elizabeth. At least one of the sisters became proficient in painting, and as can be seen from their sheet music, more than one of them was attracted by the concert performances of the day.

On the extreme right of the picture, Croquet at Brockley Hall, in front of the hedge, can be seen a gardeners thermometer.

At this time, the gardener, William Vodkins shared the gardeners cottage with his wife Susan. In July 1861 he exhibited at the Crystal Palace Rose Show, and was awarded fourth prize in his catergory.

The following year he exhibited at the Sydenham Horticultural Society, it being reported that "The prizes were very deservedly monopolised by four or five gentleman" one of whom was "Vodkins, gardener to J.T. Noakes, Esq. of Brockley Hall."

By 1870 there was a new gardener at Brockley Hall called George Fairbairn who had an under gardener called William Forsyth, a young man aged 20. One Sunday afternoon at the beginning of September George Fairbairn took an afternoon nap in the gardeners cottage. He was awoken by a loud retort, and opened his eyes to find himself bleeding from a wound to his head, and on moving towards the stairs, there was another loud bang, a gunshot causing a wound to his left shoulder, the force of which knocked him down. On being arrested, Forsyth who had shot him, claimed to have been writing a letter, when a feeling came across him and someone said to him "go and get the gun, you must shoot and kill the gardener." He later claimed he did not remember anything after he had got up to get the gun.

He had previously been employed in a nursery at Highgate where he had suffered a pain in the head, caused by working in a hot house. There had been no animosity towards gardener Fairbairn, and he had been on friendly terms. He was acquitted on the grounds of temporary insanity, and ordered to be detained during Her Majesty's pleasure. Fairbairn lived to face happier times.

At the Royal Horticultural Show of April 1871 a First Class Certificate was awarded for "Rhododendron The Bride, a superb greenhouse variety, with pure white flowers of large size, fine form, and great substance, and very freely produced, from Mr. G . Fairbairn, gardener to Mr. J.T. Noakes, Esq, Brockley Hall, Lewisham."

In the early years Brockley Hall occupied a tranquil spot in the countryside of West Kent. A dirt track led up from New Cross, past Brockley Hall, The Castle Inn, and Colgate Farm, turned to the left of Brockley Farm past a pond and then in a curve towards the only other building in the neighbourhood, a harness makers premises at Gladiator Street.

For many years the house was comparatively isolated, the nearest station being Forest Hill. However in 1871 the London Brighton and South Coast Railway opened a station which gave its name to what is now Brockley and the following year the London Chatham and Dover Railway opened Brockley Lane station on a bridge above, on what was known as the Greenwich line. As London expanded, landowners were anxious to benefit from housing construction. Estate developers paid one thousand pounds in 1886 to the London Brighton and South Coast Railway to open another station, at Honor Oak Park on 1 April that year. For a time a path of red rubble indicated the line that Stondon Park was to take, a few houses had been built in Holmsley Road, and the other turnings, which were to come much later, indicated by wooden marker fences. By 1892 Crofton Park station had been opened by the London Chatham and Dover Railway, the line skirting the grounds of Brockley Hall, and the station giving its name to the district. By 1895 Brockley was served by a single decker horse drawn bus, run by a John Partridge. The route ran from New Cross Station, along Florence Road, Rokeby Road, Brockley Road, St. Peter's Hill (probably now Geoffrey Road) Brockley Road, Brockley Lane (now Brockley Rise) and terminated near Dalmain Road School and Stanstead Road, where Tilling's buses ran from Catford. John Partridge's bus had a livery of dark green. There was a seat across the width of the roof facing towards the back behind the driver which held four passengers, and room for eight passengers inside, who boarded the bus by a door at the back. The inside passengers handed their fare to the driver through a hatch in the roof. The route from New Cross Station was three miles long, the journey time was thirty minutes, for a full fare of twopence.

In 1884 John Tompsetts's wife, Elizabeth, died at the age of 74 and he passed away in 1896, a widower for 12 years. His death certificate recording his 83 years gently describes the occasion as a "Decay of nature".

Pauline, the eldest of his five daughters died in 1906 at the age of 68.

The first tram service came in February 1911, extending the track from Brockley Cross. From June 1912 some cars terminated at a stop called Brockley Hall. The tram crews waiting in the cold by Brockley Hall, for the time of their scheduled return, were doubtless pleased to be supplied with woolly gloves and scarves knitted by, and gifted to them by the Noakes sisters.

The picture on the following page, haymaking, was taken about 1910. The property was by then hemmed in by Crofton Park Road built 1898, Stondon Park built about the same time, and within a few years completely surrounded when the lands of Colgate Farm were given over to housing. Each day Bertram Noakes could be seen setting out in his closed carriage to work, and the cows taken in for milking to the sheds near to Brockley Lane. A short walk down the footpath opposite the Brockley Jack, two high doors in the fence opened out across a little stream that ran adjacent to it, over the footpath, and after their milking, guided the cows across into the adjacent field.

The years to follow were to be sad ones for Brockley Hall. Elizabeth Noakes the

Courtesy of Lewisham Local History and Archives

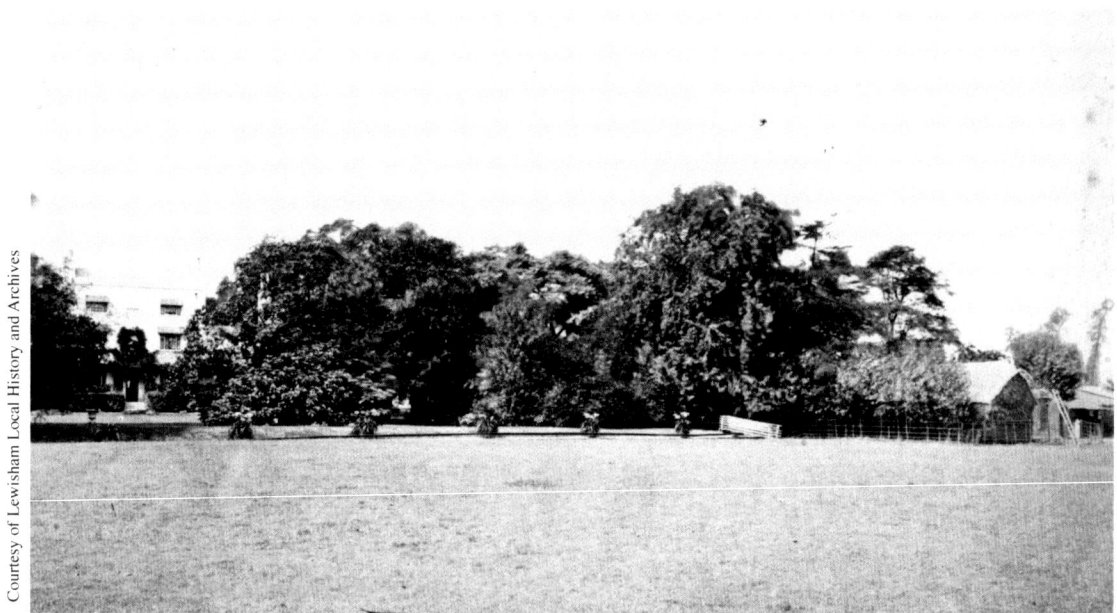

Brockley Hall the building to the left, note the haystack and farm buildings to the right - in later times known locally as Noakes Farm.

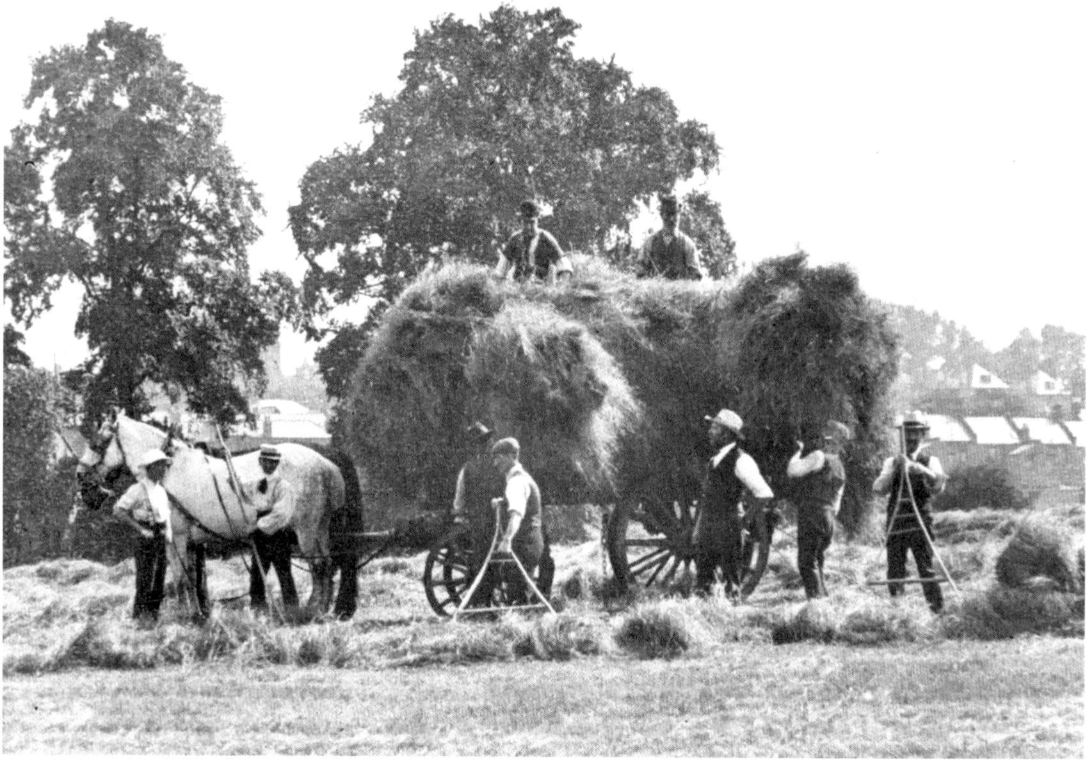
Courtesy of Lewisham Local History and Archives

Haymaking in the field opposite St.Hilda's Church about 1910.

second eldest sister, suffered a cerebral haemorrhage and passed away after two years in a coma, in 1917. Ada Louisa, the first of the sisters to be born at Brockley Hall after the family moved from Kennington in 1846, died of the same condition as Elizabeth in August 1920 and Kate who had suffered from asthma and bronchitis for several years died a few weeks later on 20 October 1920. Bertram Noakes, who had returned to live at the Hall after the death of his wife in 1919, died in the summer of 1922 at the age of 71.

Maud remained, the last of the Noakes family, in a house of ghosts. Nothing was ever thrown away, and over the years as more and more clothes and possessions accumulated, so more cupboards would be built, some even built on to the outside of other cupboards. The blinds to her room on the first floor were never drawn open, and she would be seen in the neighbourhood, sometimes on horseback, chatting by the style, more often in her carriage, in bonnet and shawl, and very particular.

One day she took a cab from Brockley station to the Hall, the cab driver wanted to charge her for over a mile, which she disputed. So she had it professionally measured. It came to 18 yards over.

She considered it her duty, in an almost manorial way, to look after the poor of the parish. If the church let her know that someone was in need, she would pull up at the address in her carriage and pair, walk straight in, and survey the scene, note anything that appeared worn or lacking. A few days later a van would deliver to that house the best Witney blankets, eiderdowns, etc... from Harrods! No one was to go in need if Maud could help it. The gates to the Hall were always open to the needy, and across the cobbled pavement with its pump, any poor person could go in to the stone floored kitchen for soup and sustenance at any time.

In her final years she had the foresight to see that so many people, the servants, gardener, driver, ex-Noakes Company employees even, relied on her for support, and that as the last of the family residing there, the future for Brockley Hall after her demise was uncertain. She added paragraph after paragraph to a will which included every conceivable benefice to all she could think of providing for. There were over thirty five beneficiaries, including pensions for servants and ex-members of staff, support for the Gospel Standard Aid Society and an annuity to provide for the poor and needy through the Zion Chapel, Malham Road.

Her last days were spent in a four poster bed of some antiquity, an old spittoon doing good service, could be discerned in the darkness behind the blinds, her life slowly succumbed to bronchial afflictions, and finally ended on 11 April 1931.

In the days following the passing of Maud Noakes the many cupboards of the house were emptied, piles of clothing were carried outside for burning, and local women were invited to take anything away. There were heaps of shoes, many unworn, out of date and unwearable. Among the ancient finery were three bridal dresses. Soon much of the Hall contents were auctioned off, and the Hall and lands gave way to the new housing of Sevenoaks Road, Bearstead Rise, Otford Crescent and Horsmonden Road. Part of the land was added to the adjacent sports field. The building itself gave its name to Brockley Hall Road.

Image courtesy of Marigold de Jongh and Lesley Yeo

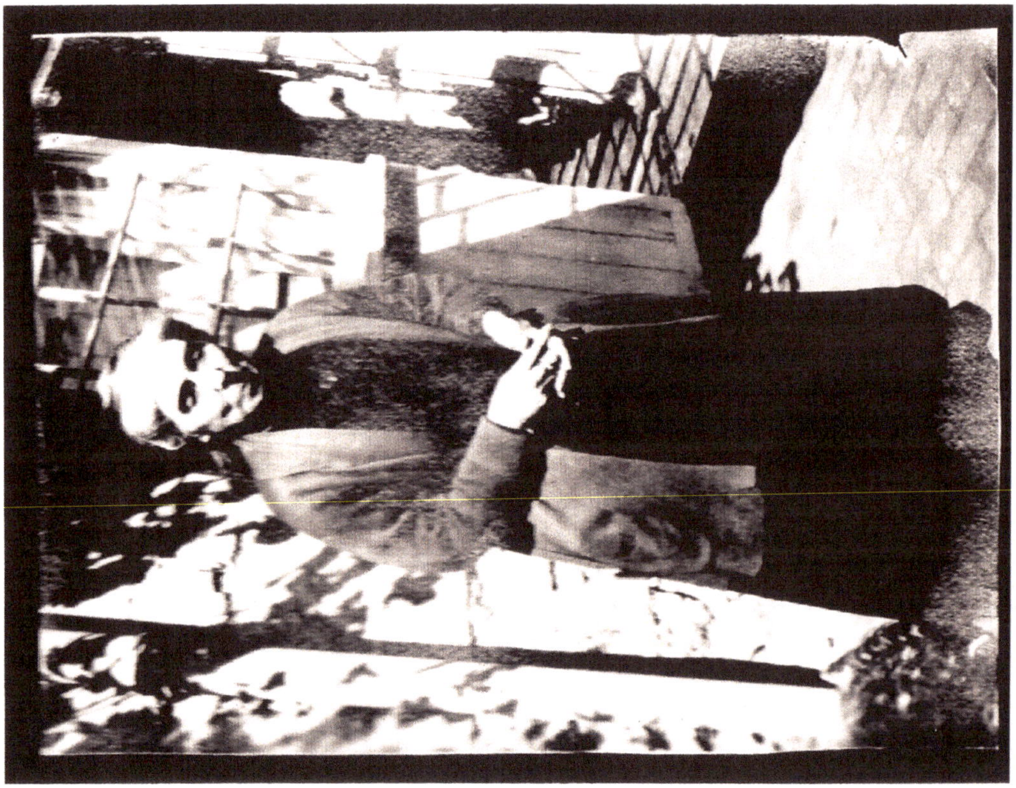

Maud Noakes 1849 - 1931 . . . the last Noakes of Brockley Hall.
" She considered it her duty to look after the poor of the parish"

Image courtesy of Lewisham Local History and Archives

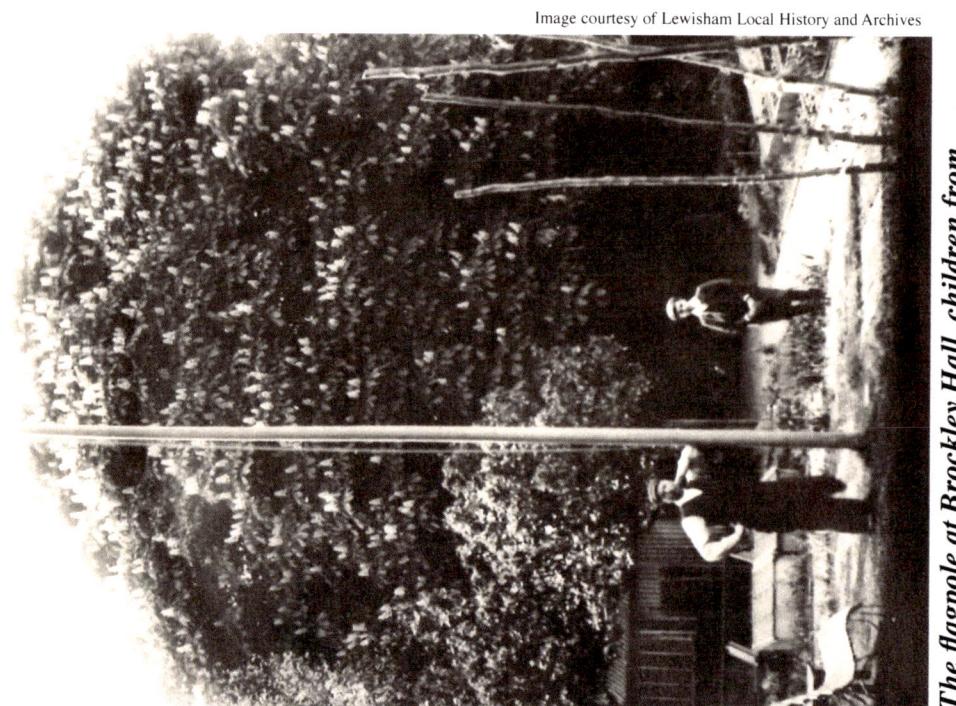

The flagpole at Brockley Hall, children from Brockley Road School would gather for the raising of the flag on Empire Day.

Music that once belonged to Bessie (Elizabeth) and Ada Louisa Noakes. Printed courtesy (copyright) Trustees of the British Museum

The two houses behind the fence to the left of this picture were known as St.Germain's Cottages, later King's Cottages and are recorded in the 1901 census as housing the Gardener to Brockley Hall, George King and his wife, next door to the Coachman, George Lamb and his son George. The ivy covered building far right is the gateway to Brockley Hall.

A variety of Noakes' pubs:-

The Dartmouth Arms - Forest Hill

The Pawleyne Arms, Penge

The Alliance, Norwood Junction

A Noakes pub - Old Kent Road

The Brockley Jack, Crofton Park

The Reindeer Inn, Slough

The Grove Park - Chiswick

Beer label

Beer label

Two Noakes bottle openers

Noakes beer bottle

Noakes fizzy drink bottle

Noakes beer bottle

A Noakes Horse Drawn Dray

A Noakes Lorry

Image courtesy of the Brewery History Society

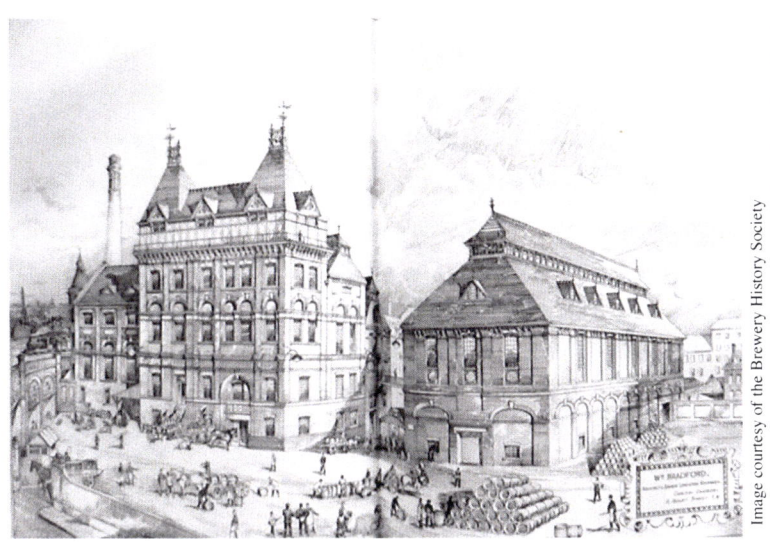

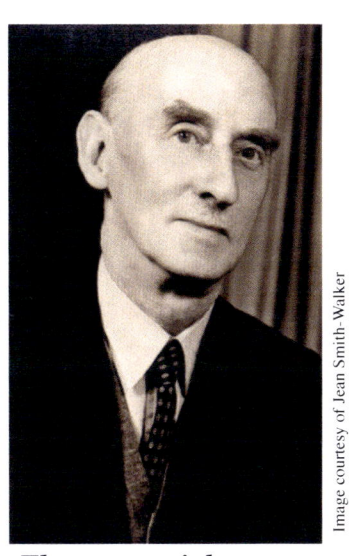

Picture of Noakes Black Eagle Brewery, Bermondsey from - The Brewers Journal 1898

Image courtesy of Jean Smith-Walker

The company's last Master Brewer J.S.Daley

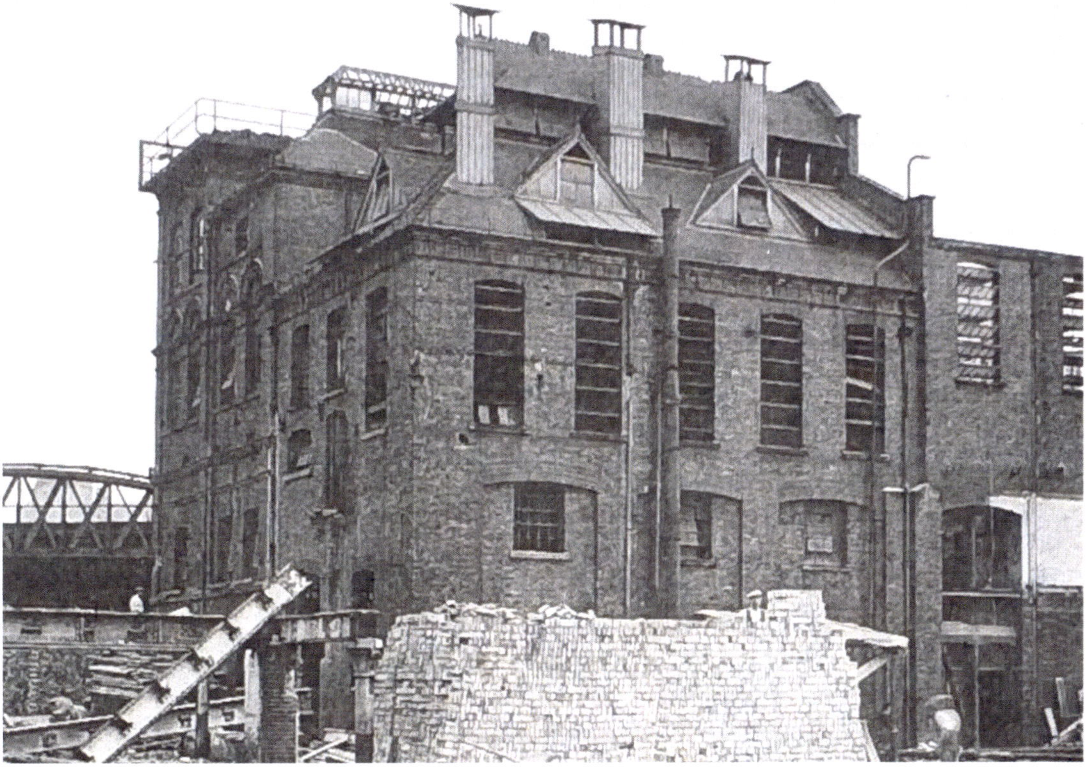

Image courtesy of Southwark Local History Library and Archives

Noakes Bermondsey Brewery during demolition

Noakes Siblings

John Tompsett Noakes had a younger brother, Benjamin Tompsett Noakes, born 1828. He married in 1850 Sarah Piper, the daughter of an engineer, and emigrated to New York, where he became a Barrister at Law. Later he took up the cloth, and became minister of St. Andrews Episcopal Church, Elyria, Ohio in 1857 for three years. He returned for another six years from 1870 to 1876, the present church was built when he was incumbent there. He died in Cayahoga, Ohio in 1904.

John Tompsett and his elder brother, William born in 1811, shared a business of Hop Factors, in Southwark Street for many years, until the partnership was dissolved in 1867 and John Tompsett became increasingly involved with brewing.

William lived for many years at a house called Brandon House, on Morden Hill pictured. John Tompsett's brother William, continued the business of Hop Factor until William's death in 1876, the firm then prospered under his son Charles Clarence, and later his grandson William. The business address was 9 Southwark Street, opposite the Hop Exchange. Here they had their offices and sample rooms of hops, where they would carry on their function of providing samples of stock from the many growers in England, and also from America, Austria, Bavaria, France and other regions renowned for this essential ingredient for brewing beer. Nearby they had three extensive warehouses, two in St.Thomas's Street and another in Guildford Street, containing many thousands of pockets of hops, from English and overseas growers.

Charles Clarence Noakes was an industrious diary writer in which he recorded his many overseas exploits. Prior to joining the family business, Charles Clarence Noakes had been sent to America to recover from ill health, and there witnessed the civil war battle of Bull Run. In 1883 he went with his wife, Mary Ann, to visit the Nile travelling to the second

Above: St.Andrews Episcopal Church,
Elyria, Ohio, built 1875

Benjamin Tompsett Noakes
Minister at Elryia.

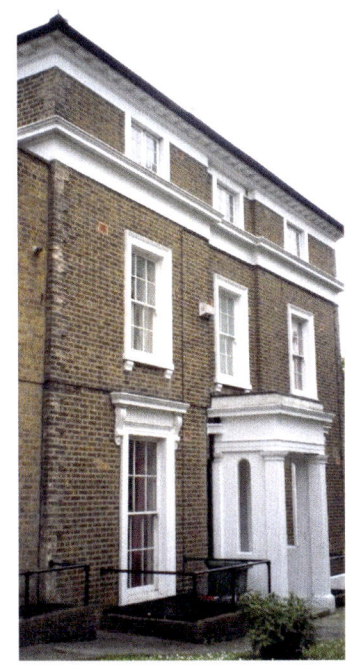

William lived for many years at a house called Brandon House, on Morden Hill pictured here.

cataract. Theirs was the last party to go up into Namibia before the campaign involving Gordon of Khartoum, and had to retreat from Wadi Halfa after the capture of Dongola by the Mahdist army. Charles Clarence lived at Ringwood, Gatton Point, Redhill, Surrey.

John Tompsett's sister, his eldest sibling, was named Ann Eliza, born in 1811, also at Ticehurst, Sussex. She married in 1836 Dr. Walter Harsant, and by 1852 she was the mother of 11 children.

In that year members of the family suffered from an out-break of scarlet fever, and as a result they decided to go abroad. They travelled to New Zealand in the 'Hamila Mitchell' the following year and settled first in TeAwamatu, and later in Raglan. Sir George Grey, the Governor of New Zealand, appointed Dr. Walter Harsant as Resident Magistrate and Colonial Surgeon. In later life they moved to Onehanga. Ann Eliza died in 1900, her husband having passed away three years previously.

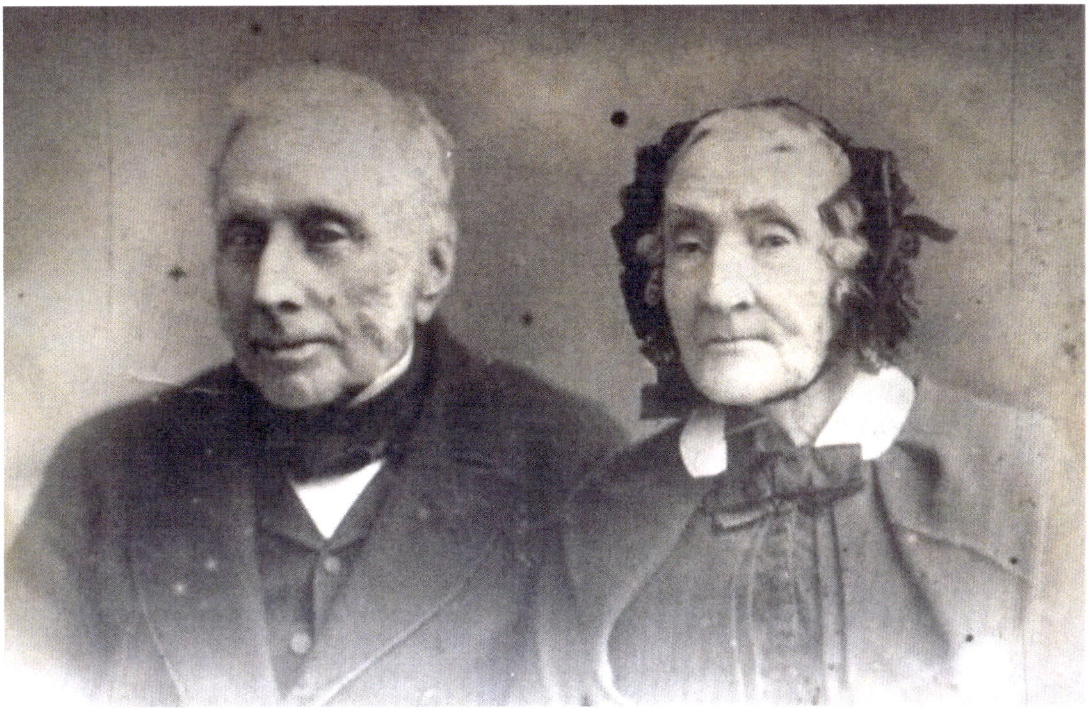

Image courtesy of the Raglan and District Museum, New Zealand

Dr.Walter Harsant ***Mrs.Harsant (Ann Eliza Noakes)***

Traces of the past

A keen eye can still discern a few reminders of history. At number 11 The Avenue, Beckenham, a block of flats now marks the spot where stood Wickham Noakes house, Fairfield, named after him as Wickham Noakes Court.

A few years after the death of Wickham Noakes, his later house Selsdon Park, was incorporated into Selsdon Park Hotel and there at the hotel can still be seen the Lounge Hall and staircase, where the banners hung depicting his Coat of Arms, and the fireplace where one can still see embossed in the fire surround, the three leopards depicted in those arms.

On top of One Tree Hill, a few yards from the oak planted in 1905, one can still see the hexagonal concrete base of the seat that surrounded the former tree stump.

On the sports fields below, near the crematorium fence and adjacent to the tennis court, can be seen a number of hawthorn trees. These mark the edge of the bed of the Croydon Canal, now just a slight dip in the ground.

The break in the pavement opposite number 95 Honor Oak Park marks what was once the entrance to Wells Fireworks factory.

In Buckthorne Road the alleyway between numbers 5 and 7 is the right of way that used to be part of Mud Lane, Colgate Farm. At numbers 5 to 8 Yates Close, Elliot Park, Blackheath, can be seen the gateway marked Cayuga, the house where Jane Colgate of Brockley Green Farm, lived with her husband Henry Robinson.

On Morden Hill can be seen Brandon House, the residence of William Noakes,the brother of John Tomsett Noakes when they were Hop Factors. Inside the Brockley Jack public house can still be seen the whale bone that once carried the inn sign that hung on a tree in the garden. Outside the entrance of what is now the Brockley Jack Theatre, can be seen the foundation stone inscribed as being laid by Wickham Francis Noakes.

Last but not least, high up on the side wall can still be seen the slogan NOAKES ENTIRE.

With Thanks

I extend my thanks to the following individuals and for the contributions made from their archives:

John Noakes, Norma Cornwell, Julian Noakes, Nobby Seymour, Alan Gibbs-Murray, Holly Church, Margaret Wilmshurst, Alan Wells, Victor Wells, Gerald Wells, Jean Smith-Walker, Lesley Yeo and Marigold de Jongh.

May I also thank Eva Wolynska for the extracts from the diaries of Elihu Burritt and Anna Strickland, for the help given by Patricia Connolly, the assistance of Anne Pickett, the computer support of Clifton Christian and for the kind consideration of Tim Joseph and Ian McAllister.

I extend my gratitude for the facilities afforded to me and the assistance of the staff of the following organisations:

London Metropolitan Archives, Southwark Local History Library and Archives, Lewisham Local History and Archives Centre, Bromley Local Studies and Archives, Museum of Croydon, Raglan and District Museum, New Zealand, Alan Godfrey Maps, Wells Fireworks, Sevenoaks Unitarian Church, Open Spaces Museum of English Rural Life, The College of Arms, Trustees of the British Museum, Central Connecticut State University, U.S.A. The Stock Exchange Memorial, The British Library, London Transport Museum, The Labologist's Society, Historic England.